All of us need people who encourage us in our gifting and spiritual life, but typically we gravitate toward our own way of relating to God and the things of the Spirit. Blake's book is a great opportunity to break away from what we are familiar with. His brilliant writing style takes his spiritual worldview and makes it accessible to us all. This book will expand your horizons, increase your hunger, and equip you for the days in which we live!

—Paul Manwaring

The Veil is a must read. I have been encouraging many people to read this extremely insightful book. In this book Blake opens up his life and takes you on a journey through his own experiences and shows how God has taught him how to steward what he sees and to partner with heaven in the process. Brilliant!

—Eric Johnson
Senior Pastor, Bethel Redding

T0059697

THE VEIL

THE
VEIL

BLAKE K. HEALY

CHARISMA
HOUSE

Most CHARISMA HOUSE BOOK GROUP products are available at special quantity discounts for bulk purchase for sales promotions, premiums, fund-raising, and educational needs. For details, write Charisma House Book Group, 600 Rinehart Road, Lake Mary, Florida 32746, or telephone (407) 333-0600.

THE VEIL by Blake K. Healy
Published by Charisma House
Charisma Media/Charisma House Book Group
600 Rinehart Road
Lake Mary, Florida 32746
www.charismahouse.com

Unless otherwise noted, all Scripture quotations are taken from the Holy Bible, New International Version®, NIV®. Copyright © 1973, 1978, 1984, 2011 by Biblica, Inc.™ Used by permission of Zondervan. All rights reserved worldwide. www.zondervan .com. The "NIV" and "New International Version" are trademarks registered in the United States Patent and Trademark Office by Biblica, Inc.™

Scripture quotations marked NASB are from the New American Standard Bible, copyright © 1960, 1962, 1963, 1968, 1971, 1972, 1973, 1975, 1977, 1995 by The Lockman Foundation. Used by permission. (www.Lockman.org)

Cover design by Vincent Pirozzi
Design Director: Justin Evans

Visit the author's website at www.blakekhealy.com.

Library of Congress Cataloging-in-Publication Data:
Names: Healy, Blake K., author.
Title: The veil / Blake K. Healy.
Description: Lake Mary, Florida : Charisma House, 2018. |
Includes bibliographical references and index.
Identifiers: LCCN 2017054772| ISBN 9781629994901 (trade
paper : alk. paper) | ISBN 9781629994970 (ebook : alk. paper)
Subjects: LCSH: Visions. | Spirits. | Powers (Christian theology)
| Gifts, Spiritual.
Classification: LCC BV5091.V6 H43 2018 | DDC 235--dc23
LC record available at https://lccn.loc.gov/2017054772

While the author has made every effort to provide accurate
Internet addresses at the time of publication, neither the
publisher nor the author assumes any responsibility for errors
or for changes that occur after publication. Further, the
publisher does not have any control over and does not assume
any responsibility for author or third-party Web sites or their
content.

23 24 25 26 27 — 11 10 9 8 7
Printed in the United States of America

For my wife, April, who has brought more freedom and love into my life than I could have ever imagined.

CONTENTS

ACKNOWLEDGMENTS

I would like to thank all of the friends and
family that have made my life
as full and rich as it is. I would like to give
special thanks to John Pitzer,
Brent Brownlee, and Dean Porter for their
help in making this book what it is.

FOREWORD

BELIEVE THAT WE are in a time of great revelation. I believe that now more than ever we need people who can see. I'm talking about those who can see physically into the realm of the spirit world. There are many in places of our society who have this unique gift. Many of them have hidden, afraid to tell what their world is like. They wonder if they are crazy. The spirit world keeps staring them in the face, and it is very real—more real than the physical world.

As we need them in our world, I always tell leaders to be open. Even though we may not walk in this gift, we need to stand up and be mentors and pastors to those who do see into the realm of the spirit.

The Bible speaks of seers. Many of the spirit leaders of the Old Testament, as well as kings, had their own seers. King David had Gad and Asaph. Saul had Samuel. Solomon had Iddo, and there are more. These leaders depended on the seers in their life; they gave them a place without abusing them.

Blake started out at a very young age. I have watched him learn and walk through this gift with its ups and downs with a lot of grace. One of the things that I love about this book is getting to see Blake's relationship with

God. His love, his revelation, and his understanding of the Father's heart will be life changing for all who read this book. Blake speaks plainly about his gift and what he went through. He talks through the good times, and the times where he hid his gift and why.

I know that I, like so many others, learn by stories. This book is filled with amazing stories of the seer world. Within these stories Blake brings out revelation and good solid truth.

One point is that being a seer is a gift that many can walk in. I found that, after reading this book, I began seeing things I had never seen before. There is an anointing in these pages for those who read with an open heart. Be prepared to receive that anointing. May an excitement rise up in you as you read the pages in *The Veil*.

The more we press into God and His wonderful presence, the more the spirit world will become alive to us.

Thank you, Blake, for bringing your life and your revelations to us. I feel this is the most insightful book on the seer anointing I have ever read.

—BENI JOHNSON
SENIOR PASTOR, BETHEL CHURCH, REDDING, CALIFORNIA
AUTHOR, *THE HAPPY INTERCESSOR*

INTRODUCTION

MY FIRST MEMORY is seeing an angel. I was two years old and buckled into a car seat in the back of my parents' minivan. My mother was in the driver's seat, chatting with the teller at a drive-through bank window. A small cluster of baseball-sized lights was drifting in the air above my mother's head. The lights swayed back and forth in time with the worship music that played on the radio, drifting like they were caught in an underwater current.

My second memory is seeing a demon. I was standing in my parents' room, straining to listen to the conversation they were having in the kitchen upstairs. Though I couldn't understand the muffled words, the unhappy tone made it clear that they were in an argument. I stared upward, hoping that would somehow make their voices come through more clearly. As I looked up, a face morphed out of the ceiling, seeping from the drywall like an over-heavy droplet of water.

Its skin was pale with dull features except for its dark eyes; it had sharp, pointed teeth and an odd, oblong head. The demon pulled free from the ceiling and drifted toward me, and I saw that everything below its shoulders was no more substantial than smoke. Not having much interest in what the flying ghoul was planning to do once it reached me, I turned and dove headlong into my parents' bed and pulled the blankets over me. After a few moments of silence, I worked up the courage to peek out from my quilted shield. It was gone.

I've seen angels, demons, and other spiritual things for as long as I can remember. I see them whenever I have the mind to look, and I see them with my eyes, just as I would see you if you were sitting in front of me.

When you're driving a car, you can look through the windshield and pay attention to the scenery, the road, and other cars (which is probably what you ought to be doing). Or you can look at the windshield itself—the glass—and all the particles of dust and water spots on it. Seeing in the spirit is not all that different. You can focus on what is happening in the physical world, or you can focus on what is going on in the spirit world.

This book represents the third attempt I've made to put my thoughts and experiences about the gift of seeing in the spirit on paper. Previous attempts were, perhaps, more in-depth and thorough. In those versions I tried to carefully dissect each experience and gather Scripture references to accompany all of my opinions. As noble as my efforts were, each attempt kept coming out overly dry and, frankly, boring. Although this could easily be blamed on my inadequacy as a writer, I felt there was more to it than that. As hope for an effective but printable version of my life experiences began to fade, God came and set me straight.

He said, "You're not trusting your readers."

And I knew He was right.

With a newfound fervor to share my experience with the world, I set out to write what I hope is a clear window into a gift I believe everyone should experience for themselves. To accomplish this, I removed most of the in-depth analysis, kept the opinions to a minimum, and added more stories.

There are clear questions that are left completely unanswered in this book. That prospect used to worry me, but I now feel that it is the best way for this to be not just a book *about* seeing in the spirit, but also an invitation. You will have to take these questions and ideas to the Lord for an answer. That may seem frustrating in the moment, but it is in service of my ultimate goal for this book, which is to challenge its readers to dive into a deeper relationship with God.

I am not a theologian. I am not a scholar. I am not a Greek or Hebrew linguist. And I have never attended seminary. Fortunately I am not trying to write to you as any of these things. My only aim is to share with you a portion of my life and let you decide what it means for yours.

With that said, there are a few simple guidelines that I feel will set you up to get the most out of this book:

1. Think: I'm not going to tell you what to think or believe about the experiences chronicled here. Some thoughts and opinions are included where I have seen fit to do so, but for the most part I'd like you to decide for yourself about these happenings. Don't worry. God wouldn't have given you such a spectacular brain unless He intended for you to put it to good use.

2. Look for good: The biggest risk I've taken in approaching this subject in this way has been asking you, my readers, to meet me halfway. In leaving room for you to draw your own conclusions about the things I've seen, I've also left room for you to make completely incorrect and negative conclusions about what I've written. Everything in this book is intended to reveal the glory of God. You may not agree with my opinions about my experiences or even the veracity of what I've seen. But this doesn't bother me as long as you come looking for the good.

3. Talk to God: Everything we think and do should be done while in conversation with God. Anything we do outside the context of relationship with Him is a complete waste of time. It is impossible to get anything beneficial from this book (or any other, quite frankly) without an intimate relationship with your Maker. He is much better at revealing Himself than I ever could be.

I realize that it is a little presumptuous to have a list of demands before starting a book, but these three requests are the biggest keys to getting the most out of it. Incidentally they are also the best way to grow in a life of seeing in the spirit. While I do want this writing to be an impartation, what I want more is for it to be an open door to God's kingdom.

MY STORY

ACT ONE

MY HANDS HAD been sweaty all day. I don't consider myself a nervous person, but I had good reason that day. I stood outside a small apartment doing my best to think about how nice the weather was. It was a cool spring evening in Redding, California, and I was very near to completing my first year at the Bethel School of Supernatural Ministry. In fact, I had just returned from my school mission trip, a big part of the final semester. It had been a year of tremendous breakthrough, particularly with my gift of seeing in the spirit, but that was the last thing on my mind as I approached the door.

When I went in, I was impressed at how many people they managed to cram into that tiny apartment—forty or so, by my best guess—and most of them were my fellow students. Upon returning from my mission trip to Mexico, I had asked one of my good friends if I could speak at her home group. Looking at all the cheerful faces scattered around the room, I was beginning to regret that decision with every inch of my being. I had spoken to larger crowds—several times larger—but never about this.

The home group started with a few acoustic worship songs. Most of my body was coated in a fine layer of sweat. I couldn't tell if this was because of the fifty mouths insistently filling the air with hot breath or because I knew what was going to happen after worship was over.

The last song ended, and my friend gave me a brief introduction. Since too many people were piled on the carpet for me to make a clean break for the door, I leaned forward in my chair and resigned myself to my fate.

I started off with the simple things, the statement I had made a thousand times before: "I've seen angels and demons for as long as I can remember. I see them as clearly as I see all of you. I can choose to focus on them whenever I feel compelled to do so."

With the simple facts out of the way, there was little left to share but what I was terrified to speak about. At that point no more than three people knew my life story, and most of them knew only bits and pieces. This was the first time I had ever told my story in its entirety.

∾

I didn't know I was seeing in the spirit when I was young. I remember seeing lights and colors swirl through the air when we went to church on Sunday. And I recall the occasional shadowy, winged creature soaring over my Southern California neighborhood, but to me they were no more fantastic or unusual than a low-flying plane or a dog walking down the street. I tried to point out these intriguing anomalies to my parents, insisting that I'd seen a dinosaur flying over our house or a man painting light on the ceiling. They paid little mind, assuming I had a colorful imagination, and I paid even less mind to their disinterest. I figured they didn't care about the dark monsters and beautiful lights, just as they didn't care about the trees, buildings, and ATM machines that my young mind found so fascinating. I had no reason to think that anything was out of the ordinary.

My parents knew God. They had been introduced shortly after I was born and had been fervently pursuing Him ever since. The church we attended didn't believe that the gifts of the Spirit were meant for today, so my parents had no reason to expect that I'd have one of the said gifts. They were intent on serving God to the fullest, however, so my dad went to Bible college, and my mom began dreaming of life as a missionary. We moved to Russia when I was five.

Our church in California and my dad's Bible college had not taught us about the presence of the Holy Spirit, but it was pouring out in Moscow. People trembled, wept, laughed, fell, stood with arms raised, danced, sang, shouted, ran, and were healed in the presence of God. I loved watching the services; lights of every color would streak across the ceiling during worship. Beautiful women wearing robes made of light and paint would run along the tops of chairs with massive banners that trailed fifty feet. Waves of crystalline water, oil, and lightning would swell through the auditorium, filling the lungs and eyes of the congregation with warmth.

The presence of God attracts the hungry as well as the hurt. Tormented by demonic voices, some people would cry out and writhe on the floor while others would shout in unnatural tones. I remember seeing men with scales growing on their necks, their eyes as red as blood. Black grime and smoke poured out of the mouths of those who had approached the stage in search of deliverance, while dark hands dug clawed fingers into the backs of the ones who couldn't summon the courage to go forward.

It was an exciting time to be in Russia. Communist

hard-liners were staging a coup outside the Russian White House backed by an ample collection of soldiers and tanks. Citizens were learning to exercise freedoms that had been suppressed for generations. None of this meant very much to a five-year-old, apart from the opportunity to watch a tank roll down the street, but I remember seeing the results of this turmoil written on the faces of people when we ministered to them.

I noticed raw sores around the necks and wrists of many of the Russians in our church. I think that these were marks left by the shackles the oppressive government had put on them. Sure, they had left many people wounded, but now the shackles were gone. I didn't understand this when I was small—at least not in the political sense—but I think part of me understood the new freedom these people were experiencing. And it gave me a great affection for the Russian people.

We ministered in Russia for three and a half years, leaving only after adopting my youngest sister from an orphanage just outside of Moscow. Many of the local laws regarding adoption by internationals were still being established at that time, so it seemed prudent to leave the country.

∾

I had no control over what I saw when I was young. Streams of light and smoky shadows flitted in and out of my vision, unbidden and without any apparent purpose. Now I can see in the spirit whenever I have the mind to look.

Before we delve more deeply into my life story, I'd like to define a few terms. I don't consider my way of thinking to be the best or only way to look at seeing in the spirit; it's just the way I organize the experiences that have dotted my day-to-day life. These terms exist less as a means of defining aspects of the spirit realm and more as a way for you to have some clue as to what I'm talking about.

THE THREE REALMS

I believe that there are three realms of existence. Some people call these the first, second, and third heavens, while some call them the physical, soul, and spirit realms. I'm sure there are many other fancy names for these concepts, but I'll refer to them as the physical, soul, and spirit realms because it makes the most sense for my purposes in this book.

The physical realm is one you ought to be pretty familiar with. It is the one that is full of all the trees, cars, buildings, mountain bikes, and beluga whales—the one in which your physical body exists at this very moment. Here you eat food, swim in the ocean, make microwave popcorn, cut your finger on a clumsily handled knife, and walk out your existence as the lifelong physical manifestation of your soul and spirit. It is a cloudy but true reflection of the other two realms.

The soul realm is where your mind, will, and emotions exist. This makes it the perfect place for demons to try to influence you, but this is also one of the places where the Holy Spirit will speak. You make all your choices here because all the experiences of the physical realm and the influences of the spirit realm pass through this tumultuous area.

The spirit realm is, honestly, still an abstract concept

for me. I think this is where God is. Sure, God is omnipresent (meaning that He is everywhere), but I think He lives in the spirit realm.

I asked God what a spirit was one day. He said that a spirit is "raw identity," the genetic code that tells everything else how to exist. Your spirit exists outside of time and is everything you will ever be. In fact, everything you are is so unique and complex that it is only fully expressed over the course of your entire life. You would probably say that you are a different person now than you were five, ten, or fifty years ago. Your spirit is all of that, all at once, and it is also everything you will ever be. Your life is an expression of the spirit that God created. Life certainly isn't perfect, but knowing that the original blueprint is always available convinces me that it most certainly could be.

WHAT IS SEEING IN THE SPIRIT?

Your physical body exists in the physical realm (in case context clues haven't led you to this conclusion). People recognize you based on your physical appearance, and you recognize them by theirs. While each of us is a spirit with a soul that lives in a body, an angel is a spirit that is not limited by physical form. When I see angels, I am seeing a visual representation of what and who they are.

For example, right now, as I sit in my living room typing away on my laptop, there is a tall angel standing next to the front door. The top of his head is an inch from touching the ceiling. He has dark brown hair combed neatly to one side and a stern glare that seems intent on completely ignoring my attention. He is built long and lean, is wearing leather armor that seems well placed for mobility, and is carrying a spear in his right hand that is as tall and straight as his posture.

This is a protection angel, here to guard my home. He looks the way he does because that reflects his purpose. Since angels are spirits not limited by physical form, and a spirit is raw identity, I am seeing a visual metaphor of who this angel actually is.

I used to say that when you see something in the spirit, you understand it. This was never entirely true, because much of what I see is obscure and confusing. A truer statement is that "You *recognize* whatever you see in the spirit." Though you may not fully understand it, there is a familiarity that comes when you see. Perhaps this is because even though we spend most of our attention on the physical realm, we exist in the spirit realm every minute of every day.

∾

Apart from the odd looks I received when pointing out things that no one else saw, I never had a reason to think anything was out of the ordinary. I liked the bright lights and glorious beings that filled my house and church. When demonic entities came clawing at our car windows or peered behind the eyes of the brokenhearted, I never felt any real danger. It was as though I was viewing the spirit world through a thick layer of bulletproof glass. Any demon I saw was no more threatening than a caged lion at the zoo. But that all changed when I turned nine.

After four years as missionaries, my parents decided it was time to go home. Rather than return to the sunny shores of Southern California, we moved to Holland, Michigan. It was the perfect kind of quaint and quiet town for a family in need of respite. We moved into a small house on Church Street, and I started my first semester in an American school.

I distinctly remember walking onto the playground during the first recess of fourth grade. As I surveyed the landscape littered with my fellow elementary students, I contemplated a life among a hundred children who were just like me. Giving a sigh of satisfaction at the prospect of living a life as normal as any of them, I ran to join a game of handball. I paid no mind to the dozen or so winged men with golden spears flying over the school grounds.

I don't know if it was because I was now among peers who shared the same language or simply because I was growing older, but it wasn't long before I realized something was off. It happened slowly. Though I had seen it a dozen times before, it suddenly seemed odd that my teacher came into class with deep cuts on her face. I also began to realize that no one talked about the stoic figures who stood vigil night and day at the school entrance. In fact, no one ever mentioned any of the men who guarded certain people's houses or the pretty lady who walked up and down the school halls, putting oil and flowers on the heads of everyone she passed. Not even the black dog as big as a house that floated over the city drew attention from anyone apart from myself. Before suspicion could turn into understanding, my world changed.

I was lying in my bed about to fall asleep, and my door was open just enough to let a crack of light cut across the carpet. I watched the light flicker as my parents walked back and forth down the hall. Just as sleep was about to overtake consciousness, someone stopped in the doorway. Thinking it was my mother checking if I was asleep, I turned to look.

A shadow, less substantial than fog but more solid than air, slid through my cracked door. It was the vaguest shape of a man, little more than a head on a pair of indistinct shoulders. It moved across the room, coming to rest at the foot of my bed.

I had seen dark beings more frightening in appearance than this shadow—sallow, sharp-toothed beasts with yellow eyes and slimy horrors with broken bones jutting from their rotten flesh. There had, however, always been a sense of separation whenever I found myself in the presence of such creatures. Their hateful glares and gnashing teeth seemed like something on television—scary, but certainly nothing that could ever touch me.

As this shadow reached the foot of my bed, his eyes flashed—white blurs floating somewhere in the smoky head—and I felt fear.

I wasn't afraid that I was going to die. I wasn't afraid that he was going to hurt me. I wasn't afraid of anything in particular. I was simply surrounded and filled with absolute and complete fear. My body froze. My gaze locked on those empty, white eyes. The fear had no focus, no idea with which to torment me. It was a fear so cold and all-consuming that my mind had no room for anything but absolute terror. It felt as though huge leather straps had been laid across my chest, both holding me in place and crushing my lungs. I don't know how long I was stuck like that—somewhere between ten seconds and three hours. Eventually I managed to roll over and fall asleep, facedown on my pillow. The shadow was gone when I woke the following morning.

Everything seemed normal enough the rest of the next day. Around town and at school I saw the regular demons that I'd seen every day before, and I wasn't afraid when I saw them. The bulletproof glass that kept me feeling safe was back. I decided that the unpleasantness of the previous night had simply been an unusually tangible nightmare—that is, until I found the shadow waiting at the foot of my bed that night. My mother tucked me in and kissed me good night, but I was too busy staring at those cold, white eyes to pay her much notice. The eyes flashed the moment she left the room, and I found myself drowning in absolute terror once again. It was half an hour before I could roll onto my face to fall asleep.

Being a reasonably fast learner, when I found the shadow waiting in my room on the third night, I put on my pajamas and lay down face first onto my pillow without looking at the white eyes. I wish it had been that simple. The fear came again, this time as cold, moist breath running up my legs, along my spine, and around my neck. It still paralyzed me, but it no longer wiped my mind free of thought. Instead it flooded my head with horrible images.

I saw hundreds of people standing naked in a line, waiting to be tortured by some disfigured abomination of a man. A small boy was being thrown into a pit full of dead and dying men, women, and children who were all fighting to keep from being smothered by the density of filthy flesh. It was as if I was being shown footage from some hellish concentration camp. This went on every night for a few days, and the film wouldn't stop until I fell asleep. Finally I couldn't bear it. I pulled my face away from the pillow to look at my shadowy tormentor, only to find that the images that had filled my mind were now swarming around my room in full 3D Technicolor.

From then on, a procession of new horrors decorated my bedroom every night. More twisted and evil images than my nine-year-old mind could have constructed or even comprehended appeared with increasing intensity. Scenes of death, torture, and violent sexual depravity played out across the floor, walls, and ceiling of my room like some malevolent ballet. At first I was so horrified I couldn't look away, but after a few weeks all I wanted to do was clamp my eyes shut. Even then the visions would just crawl underneath my eyelids, so I still saw them, even with my eyes closed.

I started playing worship music at bedtime—Amy Grant tapes, if I remember correctly. It helped numb the sting of dread that left me paralyzed nightly, but it did little else. After a week or two the tape player stopped working at night, even though it functioned perfectly during the day. The docile tones would quickly dissolve into indistinct static just minutes after my head hit the pillow. One night the music faded away almost instantly, and after a minute of static a new song began to play. It was a horrible broken violin sound, scratching out a homicidal tune that sent icicles down my spine. I leapt out of bed and yanked the power cord out of the wall, but the music continued to play for another five minutes.

So these horrors continued, night after night, for three years. Each night seemed worse than the last. Sometimes my walls were coated in thick layers of rotten meat crawling with every kind of multi-legged creep. On other occasions I'd simply be witness to a demonic figure continuously ripping himself to pieces and then putting himself back together in odd ways, only to begin violently disassembling himself again. I'd often see several sets of long, sinuous hands reaching out from under my bed. They'd grab the sheets in various places looking for something to sink their cracked claws into. Every night I would face some new terror.

Everything went back to normal during the day. I'd see angels and demons wherever I went, but that sense of separation shielded me from any fear—at least until the sun went down. Panic would run through my chest as bedtime approached. Cold sweat coated my back and arms as I slipped under the covers. Every cell in my body was struggling to escape the approaching fear, scrambling like millions of mice trapped in a sinking ship. I was certain that I was going crazy, though I took some solace in the knowledge that being aware of the threat of insanity made me slightly less insane.

Naturally my parents began to suspect that something was wrong. I realized, however, that seeing a cornucopia of malice pour into my room every night wasn't the surest sign of sanity, so I never shared the full extent of my nighttime horrors with them. I only said that I was scared at night, and they did everything that one would expect from good Christian parents. They prayed with me, told me what to pray, and let my sister sleep on the couch in my room. But no matter what I prayed, nothing changed. Speaking the name of Jesus felt like throwing sand at a hurricane, and singing "God has not given me a spirit of fear" only made the demons laugh.

Having my sister, Bree, sleep on the couch next to my bed helped a little, but only because I could look at the angels who huddled around her while she slept. I would occasionally sneak into my parents' room and crawl halfway under their bed to escape the contents of my room. Everything I tried only worked for a short time. Nothing stemmed the tide of terror that drowned me each and every night.

∽

After three and a half years of living in Michigan, my parents decided it was time to move back to California to be closer to the rest of our family. Some part of my heart, for reasons I couldn't explain, believed that this transition would bring change to the inescapable spiral of fear I had been trapped in for three years. Hope, indistinct as it was, dulled the pain of my visions. Though the weeks leading up to our departure held some of the worst of the nightly horrors, I couldn't help feeling that there was now a light at the end of my tunnel.

PART I
DEMONS
AND SUCH

T's A TUESDAY night, and it is hot in the sticky way that the state of Georgia becomes all too often. I'm sitting in a chocolate-brown microsuede reading chair that was clearly chosen by someone who cared more about quaint charm than comfort. The smell of burnt coffee beans mingles nicely with the vaguely European jazz interrupted only by the occasional sharp hiss of steam.

A girl with long, wavy brown hair sits at the table across from me. She is the typical twenty-something-sitting-by-herself-with-a-laptop-in-a-coffee-shop kind of girl. A demon is creeping up her back—a sniveling, pathetic looking thing with bony limbs and dead, gray skin. It's almost human in shape but no bigger than a cat, with a noseless face and wet hands.

It starts at the leg of her chair, the look on its face a strange perversion of a two-year-old taking a tentative step toward an open cookie jar. She doesn't react as the demon puts a hand on her leg. As if this is the signal to go, the demon hops onto the back of the chair and with twitching fingers grabs a small handful of her hair in its oily palms.

Now the girl reacts—whether she realizes it or not—reaching back and running her fingers over the spot where the demon grasped. The black oil from the demon's hand, which was almost invisible in her dark hair, is all too plain on her otherwise clean fingers.

A look of frustration cuts across her face. She pinches the bridge of her nose with dirtied fingers, and then runs

19

them along her cheek, leaving smears all the way. It's subtle, but I see the look on her face move from frustration to sadness for the briefest of moments. The demon sees this better than I do, seizing the opportunity to lean in and whisper something into her ear. I can't hear what he's saying or read his lipless mouth, but I know what he said: "You're not good enough. No one loves you. You're not worth it. This always happens to you." He tells her the same accusations that assault all of our minds daily.

Fortunately the girl isn't having any of it. She shakes off the sadness almost as quickly as it comes, straightening her shoulders with a deep breath that sends the demon tumbling off the back of the chair. It skitters away with folded arms and a hurt look in its eye. I am happy to see her shake off the lies, but the girl's face still has those smudges. I imagine they will stay until she decides that they don't belong.

Movies, overzealous preachers, and an underdeveloped sense of identity in Christ have caused many misconceptions about demons. Some think that the world is stuffed full of evil forces poised and ready to pounce the moment you pick up that heavy metal album or step into that horror movie. Others think that the only thing holding back the torrent of darkness that aches to pour into your life is a healthy diet of good deeds and teeth-gritting resistance to temptations of the flesh and eyes.

The truth is that demons are more attracted by what you think than what you do. The deeper truth is that knowing who you are in Christ determines how you think. The only way to know who you are in Christ is to know what He thinks about you. That is to say, if you know what God has to say about you, then the lies of the enemy seem silly. This is the majority of what you need to know about dealing with demons.

The girl in the coffee shop didn't do anything wrong. Maybe she saw a friend say something bad about her on Facebook, maybe she got frustrated at a homework assignment, or maybe it was just the end of a hard day. Whatever the reason, the demon was attracted to her distress not because he wanted to tempt her to commit some sin but because he wanted to use that moment as an opportunity for accusation.

The demonic tries to hold our mistakes in the air as proof that we have failed as children of God. It's ironic since Jesus came and died so that our inadequacies would no longer be capable of keeping us apart from Him. I think that's why He tells us in 1 Corinthians 14:1 to pursue prophecy. If you know what God has to say about you, then it doesn't matter what anyone or anything else has to say.

∾

I was twelve when we moved back to California. The church we had been attending in Michigan believed in the gifts of the Spirit but did very little to activate them in its members. Occasionally someone would stand up during a quiet moment in worship, say a few "spiritualish" sentences, and then sit back down so that worship could continue. That was the prophetic as I knew it.

The church we attended in Southern California, however, took a very different approach. There the prophetic was something to be taught and learned, practiced and perfected. It wasn't a weird thing that haphazardly reared its head at arbitrary intervals. It was the expression of a real relationship with a living God.

It wasn't long before my very prophetic mother dragged me to the prophetic meetings held at our new church. After spending a few weeks acclimating to this new culture, I realized that my nightly displays were not the signs of steadily slipping sanity but the bumbling of an individual who was unaware of his gift.

No one at the church saw things the same way I did, but being around people who were actively pursuing a deeper understanding of the voice of God made it plain that the prophetic they were describing was intrinsically linked with the things I saw. It may not explain why I had such terrible, open visions every night, but at least it did create some context for it. This gave me the courage to share the full gravity of my nightly experiences with my parents and the prophetic leaders.

Much to my surprise, this new openness marked an almost complete halt to my evening attacks. I realized the night horrors were not happening *to* me but instead a tool I had yet to gain control over, like a rookie firefighter learning to wrangle a wildly whipping fire hose. Beginning the process of honing my ears to the voice of God equipped me to repel the attack.

After I made this discovery, it took a mere week for the demonic visions to end completely, and in that final week they lost their sting. What had been an overwhelming freak show of malevolent terror was now about as frightening as marionettes made from old Halloween decorations.

I believe that praying and speaking the name of Jesus, as I had done before this revelation, was ineffective against my demonic assailants because I was speaking out of ritual rather than authority. I only said, "Leave me alone in the name of Jesus," and I sang, "God has not given me a spirit of fear," because it was what my Sunday school teachers and parents told me to do.

Much like the sons of Sceva from Acts 19, I was speaking the name and singing the words because I *heard* they were powerful, not because I knew what they meant. I had accepted Christ into my heart at the age of three, but I never truly had a tangible relationship with Him. Being around people who heard the voice of God at our church in Southern California made it easy to *experience* the truth of His goodness and begin a real personal relationship with Him.

Knowing who God says you are is just as important as knowing who God is. It's all well and good if you see God as the all-powerful man in the sky with a lightning bolt in each hand and a white beard that reaches to His toes, but none of that does you any good if you don't know what He thinks about you. I had attended church my whole life. I had heard that God loved me and had been told I was His child a thousand and one times in a thousand and one ways. But I didn't connect with what that actually *meant* until I realized that God wanted to talk with me daily.

For the first time in my living memory I had experienced what it felt like to be a child of God. I only grasped a corner of this massive truth, but even that small piece completely transformed the way I approached life. Jesus died so that you could be a coheir with Him. If you don't believe me, read Galatians 4—the first seven verses lay it out nicely. Our Christian life is designed to be an expression of how good that truth is.

∽

Now you may be thinking, "Wait a minute. The title of this section has the word *demons* in it. What's with all this 'I'm a child of God' stuff?" I'm approaching from this angle because if you can't view the demonic from the perspective of heaven, you will only confuse yourself and waste your time. If you don't know the truth of who you are in Christ and if you don't know that you are seated in heavenly places (Eph. 2:1–7), then you are just a little boy shivering under his covers at night. But if you know what Jesus's sacrifice has won you, if you know even a piece of what God thinks about you, then you have the answer to every problem that crosses your path.

KEEPING IT PERSONAL

EMONS DON'T LIKE you. Any demon that finds you in its sights is going to do everything in its power to steal, kill, and destroy everything good about your life. The nice thing is, for the most part, this isn't really a big deal.

The fact is, the world is covered in nasty, disgusting germs that would like nothing more than to infect your body, kill you, and eat you for dinner. The reason that most of you are not in the belly of billions of bacteria is that your body is quite excellent at repelling the millions of daily attempts against your life without even noticing. Your spirit is much the same.

It would be a big waste of your time to go through life with a can of disinfectant in each hand, spraying every surface within view in fear of the day when one of those nasty little germs might penetrate your sanitizer-soaked skin. It would be an equally big waste of your time to go through life hiding from every dark corner and street musician in fear of what demonic forces may lie within. For the most part, your spirit is quite adept at repelling attacks without your notice.

Every now and then, usually when you haven't had enough sleep or have too much stress at work, one of those germs sneaks in and makes you sick. Health is the natural state of the human body—sickness is the exception. Health is also the natural state of the human spirit.

Now if you're going to use your immune system as an excuse to eat raw meat out of a back-alley garbage can, you may be missing the point. However, if you're living a life connected to God and making decisions that protect that connection, the demonic should rarely factor into your life.

WOUNDS

There was a man who attended the same prophetic group I did when I was thirteen and still coming to terms with my newly discovered talents. We'll call him Chuck, since that's not his real name, and I don't think I actually know anyone named Chuck. So Chuck was a nice guy, but he was one of those people who always had something to say. Any time there was an opening for prayer requests, he had a list. Every time he prophesied, he did so at the top of his lungs. And whenever I entered into conversation with him it quickly distilled into a long description of his weekly woes. You all probably know a Chuck or two.

Despite the general liking I have for humanity as a whole, Chuck bothered me. I didn't hate him or anything, but I wouldn't have minded if he found another prophetic group—maybe one in India or something. When I looked at Chuck in the spirit, I saw cuts and scars all along his face. They were different lengths and depths each time I saw him. Sometimes there would be one long, deep cut from his nose down to his jaw, and he'd ask for prayer because his son was doing drugs again. Other times a thick, red scar would appear along his cheek, and he'd tell the story about his ex-wife for the third time. Sometimes there would be clusters of scratch marks spread all across his face, and he'd dissolve into tears talking about how life was just too overwhelming. I would have felt sorrier for him if this weren't a weekly occurrence.

One week, while doing my best to ignore the bleeding slice that cut across his left eye, I was inexplicably drawn to a spot at the center of his chest. Though he was thoroughly clothed, I could see through his shirt to a dark bruise at the center of his sternum. It was no bigger than a golf ball and had dark blue and green rings emanating from a navy-blue center. As soon as I saw the bruise, a picture flashed through my mind.

I saw a little boy, no older than ten, crying with his chin pressed to his chest. The boy's father was standing over him, veins popping and eyes bulging—livid.

He grabbed the boy's chin and jerked it up, shouting, "Look at me!"

The boy cringed and cried all the harder.

Taking his hand off the boy's face, the father yelled, "You stop it! You stop that crying," punctuating the last three words with hard, two-fingered pokes to the boy's chest. "Nobody wants to hear you blubber on all day. You stop that NOW!" he shouted, with one final jab at the same spot.

I was never as bothered by Chuck after that. I felt as if I should say something to him, like there was a way to break the words that his father had thumped into his chest, but I never did. I was only thirteen, but even then it made me sad to see what one man's words could do. I imagine that if Chuck knew what his Father in heaven had to say about him, things would be quite different.

Wounds are, sadly, something I see on people all the time. I see them almost every day. Whether it's from your boss being disappointed with a project you put your heart into, your wife snapping at you because you forgot to pay the water bill, or just another off-kilter look from that person you're trying to be friends with—we hurt each other. You can pretend it isn't there or that it didn't bother you, but you know if it did.

Not all wounds are the same, of course. Some fade away within hours; others heal into scars that never fully leave. And still others are not allowed to heal, festering into rotten gashes that corrupt muscle and bone. How these wounds affect you is, fortunately and unfortunately, entirely up to you. I've met people who have let one idle word drag them into a dark pit of unforgiveness, bitterness, and self-pity, while others turn a past full of abuse and shame into a crown of glory by giving it over to the One who died to heal every hurt.

∾

I knew a woman on the prophetic team who was very talented. She had a natural gift for hearing the voice of God and showed great authority when she told people all the good things God had to say about them. Despite this, I couldn't help but notice the faint line that ran from her right ear to the corner of her mouth. It didn't look like

much—hardly more than a thin strip of irritated skin—
yet it never seemed to improve.

One day we were prophesying together over a middle-
aged man with a pornography problem. Statistics suggest
that his situation wasn't unusual, but this man's problem
was more evident than most. I could see the demon hop-
ping in circles around his head, poking at different places
on his face, smiling as it did. Although I've seen demons
of perversion attack plenty of people, it certainly doesn't
mean all those people had problems with immorality. It
just means that the devil wanted them to have problems
with immorality. I could tell this man had a problem
because of the look of shame that came to his face every
time the demon touched him.

I didn't know what to say to the man. Now I know I
should have told him he was a man of honor and integrity
and that God had made him to be an example of purity,
which was true. My talented, prophetic partner, however,
seemed to know exactly what she wanted to say to him.

Her face grew redder and redder with each measured
breath, and then she opened her mouth to speak. The line
that ran from ear to mouth split open, causing her jaw
to swing loose and hang from one hinge. The fleshy bits
underneath were full of maggots and rot. By this point I
had been aware of my gift for a few years, so I was quite
accustomed to seeing both shockingly grim and breath-
takingly beautiful things appear out of nowhere. I also
rarely reacted externally to their appearance. But this
time I jumped, probably because I genuinely hadn't been
expecting it.

She proceeded to give the man a "prophetic word" about

how he needed to change his ways and that opportunities were passing him by because he wasn't able to see them. As she spoke, I tried my best to figure out what had caused that extreme spiritual and verbal reaction. I was perplexed until I noticed that the demon was floating directly between my friend and the person she was prophesying to, causing her to see through the demon as if it were a filter. Seconds after I noticed the odd staging of the scene, the demon hovered into my line of sight, in front of the man.

Through the demon the man's features were subtly exaggerated and twisted in sinister fashion. Even I began to feel a measure of contempt rise in my stomach. I had to actively choose to connect with what God was saying about the man to keep the religious beast that was churning in my stomach from condemning him.

My partner somehow managed not to delve too far into the accusatory realm, but the man sure didn't look very encouraged after hearing what she had to say. I found out some time later that she had been in a very abusive marriage several years prior. It made me sad that even though she got remarried to a great man and had three wonderful children with him, that abusive relationship still left its mark on her life. Wounds that go untended skew our view, not only of those around us but also ourselves.

While part of the strategy of the demonic is to deceive us into believing lies about ourselves, the other part is trying to get us to believe lies about others. I don't know why we feel the compulsion to condemn. Maybe it makes us feel better about ourselves, or perhaps our sense of justice becomes tweaked by our own wounds. Whatever the reason, this is not how God treats people. He sent His Son to die and erase our sins from the record.

DEMONS AND INFLUENCE

Demons have no authority over you unless you give it to them. A demonic entity has no right to act in your life without expressed agreement from you. Showing up with a red pitchfork in one hand and a contract in the other is probably not going to win the devil too many souls, so instead he must look for soft soil in which to plant lies and deceit.

Once a woman came to our church who liked to prophesy during worship. Generally this wouldn't have been an issue. The problem was with the words she spoke: "Feel the magic of His breath course through your bosom," "Can you taste His power flowing from the earth?," and "Submit your will to His advances and let yourself be taken by Him."

It may seem rich for the guy who talks about demons morphing out of ceilings to pass judgment on someone saying strange words during a church service, but the feeling that emanated from what she said was even more bothersome than the words themselves.

The leaders asked her to stop. She didn't, so they asked her a little more firmly. She stopped for a week, and then she started up again. After a few weeks of this song and dance, they asked me to look at her to see what was going on.

I saw a metal clasp around her neck. It had a black chain that hung between her and a demon that sat on her shoulder. The demon was bony and pointed with thin wings and a gaunt face, standing no more than two feet tall. The demon sat on its haunches, picking at her hair like a pet monkey, until there was a pause in the worship music. Then it pulled its long hands from her hair and jabbed at her neck with a pointed finger. It must have always poked the same spot, because a red, raw hole about as big around as a pencil had been dug out of the side of her neck.

When it poked, she winced as if some part of her was trying to resist, but then she immediately began sharing her tainted words. I saw them drifting out of her mouth—glitter-dusted flower petals floating in a sickly green haze, dancing the line between pleasant and putrid. I guessed that if I could smell what I saw, it would smell like the overbearing potpourri you find in a funeral home bathroom—deception trying to hide under a sheepskin of revelation.

Our worship leader, having had his fill of the woman's weekly declarations, slammed everything into full swing with a few hard chords that drowned out the "prophetic word." The congregation seemed to appreciate his stance on the situation because everyone immediately joined in, singing at the top of their lungs. The presence of God came quickly and tangibly, bringing a warm weight to the air.

The demon's look of indignation matched the flushed anger that cut across the woman's face. It jammed its finger deep into her neck, making her visibly jump. At that moment I wondered how a demon could exist in an atmosphere so thick with the presence of God. Just then, worship swelled to a new height. The demon's look of anger melted into one of abject terror. It leapt from the woman's shoulder, flapping its wings wildly.

Then I noticed the chain that hung from the woman's

neck was attached to a clasp around the demon's wrist. It yanked at the chain frantically, clawing at the trapped wrist with its free hand. The demon was just as tied to the woman as she was tied to it.

Our fears, grudges, and wounds let demons in; and our fears, grudges, and wounds make it impossible for them to leave. These pains and attitudes may seem insurmountable at times, and that is because they are. I've seen enough moldy bandages and porcelain masks attempting to hide deep-seated wounds to know that our own efforts at repairing the damages of life are tragically inadequate. We need a love that is perfect to cast all fear from our lives. It is impossible to forgive the trespasses against us without the wisdom and comfort of the One who forgave every sin that would ever exist.

∼

The last thing I want you to do after reading this part of the book is get all introspective and insecure about your imperfections. When you accepted Christ into your heart, you became a new creation—*literally* a new creation. I've seen it happen. A blueprint has been drawn in your spirit, and you are in the process of building that perfect temple. You are the exact person God designed you to be, and you are also a work in progress at the same time.

I think some people believe we are in a process that leads to our eventual perfection, which most of us assume can't happen until we die. The more time I spend talking to God about His people, the more I've come to believe that the process itself *is* perfection.

Your inner healing and spiritual growth are secondary to your relationship with God. It's easy to get so caught up with trying to heal your internal wounds that you forget to build your relationship with the Healer. It is also easy to get so ambitious in the pursuit of gifts and anointing that you forget that your Father is the Giver. More often than not, getting rid of demonic influence is as simple as hearing what God has to say about your life.

A friend of mine came to me feeling depressed. She had a short list of things rolling around in her mind, but none of them seemed to be a very good reason for her current mood. At this point in my colorful career, I decided not to share when I saw demonic beings pestering people since I had never gotten a positive response from doing so in the past. So I didn't mention the depression demon I saw floating behind her. I'm usually pretty adept at hiding my spiritual glances, but my friend knew me too well.

"What?" she asked, staring straight into my eyes.

"What?" I responded, looking away.

She rolled her eyes. "What do you see?"

"See?" I asked, doing my best to act casual.

"Blake, if something is making me depressed, it would help me a lot if you just told me."

Now chances are that most of you are siding with my friend at the moment, but you have to understand that this was very difficult for me. Relationships had been severed, leaders had been offended, and people had spiraled into an introspective hole all because of me describing demonic activity. They always said things like "It's OK—I can handle it" or "I just really want to know." Most of the time telling them only resulted in them feeling tainted.

All this ran through my head as my friend continued to glare unflinchingly at me. Then I felt the Holy Spirit, and I knew it was OK.

"I see a demon," I said. "It's a giant eyeball that has a long, sharp nose like a mosquito, little bird legs, and insect wings. It's about as big as a grapefruit."

"Is it my fault that it's here?" she asked, finally breaking her one-sided staring contest.

"No, but it wants you to think so," I said because it's what the Holy Spirit said.

"What do I have to do to make it leave?"

It was gone before she asked the question.

Lies are the only real power demons have, and lies are only powerful if you believe them. If I hadn't had this exchange with my friend, I may never have seen the value of pointing out the enemy's hand. (And I probably would never have written this section of the book.) Now I know that there is freedom in revealing deception to be deception. As I said before, I don't want you to get all freaked out about whether you are listening to the enemy or not, but I do want to give you a few keys that I've found to be quite helpful when it comes to taking your thoughts captive:

- There is a handy list of qualities that you should look for in everything you say and do. If your thoughts create love, joy, peace, patience, kindness, goodness, faithfulness, gentleness, and self-control, then you are headed in the right direction. That may seem

35

like a lot to remember, but thankfully God was kind enough to have it written down in Galatians 5:22–23.

- Just follow rule number two from the introduction of this book. When you look for the good in every situation, it's hard for the devil to twist your perspective.

- Think about your thoughts. Think about why you feel the way you do. Why are you offended? Why are you sad? Why are you mad? This gives God a chance to speak to you about what you're thinking.

- Most importantly, make everything in your life part of your pursuit of God. A mind that is captured by the wonder of God has no room for anything else.

HOME AND HABITAT

O NE DAY WHEN I was sixteen I was doing street ministry at Venice Beach with my youth group. Venice
Beach is an interesting place, where booths dishing
out everything from free psychic readings to pamphlets
about doomsday prophecies are walled in by dirty sand
and dirtier water. Opposite this is an endless parade of
head shops, inner-city chapels, and art galleries. I really
like it there. You've never met so many open people. Sure,
plenty of them are blown out on drugs, deep into the
occult, or looking for a pocket to pick, but the majority
have come to the realization that they are in need of
something to fill their lives, which is more than can be
said for most people. This kind of nondiscriminating
spirituality leaves the door open for the demonic, but it
also leaves the door open for the Holy Spirit.

Our goal for the day was quite simple—do a little shopping and pray along the way. We had been serving at an
inner-city outreach in downtown Los Angeles, and this
was our recreation time. We walked along the beach, half
our group looking like sheep at a wolf convention. After
half an hour or so, I suddenly had the impulse to look in
the spirit. Some people are surprised when they discover
that I'm not tuned into the spirit realm constantly. While

I can see whenever I feel like looking, I usually don't look unless I feel a pull from the Holy Spirit. I don't necessarily think it's wrong to look in the spirit arbitrarily—sometimes I do—but I've found that my time is best spent looking at what God points out.

The spiritual scene was not all that different from the physical one. I noticed a colorful mixture of clean light and filthy clouds swirling together but never quite mixing. The sky resembled a beehive with each bee dressed more flamboyantly than the last. Demonic entities swam through the thick air with stained-glass wings and spindly, wrought-iron legs. Every one was a unique fabrication. It was beautiful in a disconcerting way, like watching a group of hammerhead sharks encircle a school of fish. The angels were similar—each looked as if a different artist had drawn it. They soared through the murky air, distributing inspiration wherever they saw an open mind.

A lady at a psychic booth on my left wore beautiful golden glasses with ornate detailing around the rims and inlaid jewels in the corners. They were dirty, tarnished, dented, and chipped—a gift from God kept apart from His care. This woman wasn't listening to demons, as some Christians believe of psychics; she was merely operating out of an irrevocable God-given gift.

Certainly there are people who listen to demonic voices to get inspiration for their predictions, but in my experience these are in the minority. I imagine that this woman used her gift to discern circumstances in people's lives and repeat the information back to them. If she were connected to the Holy Spirit, she would have the answers to every problem laid before her, not to mention the encouragement and grace to grow past said problems. Without it she was trying to navigate a cruise liner at midnight with a flashlight. Her limited view lacked the influence of the Holy Spirit's infinite perspective. Prophetic words and psychic readings are the same thing, if we're operating solely from the gift and not using that gift from a place of relationship with God.

Past the woman at the psychic booth was a man with a scraggly beard and a furious tan who was selling homemade bracelets and necklaces. On top of his otherwise-bald head was a dark and slimy creature. It looked something like an ink-soaked octopus with four slick arms that reached down and around the man's face and into his beard. The thing oozed inky secretions from every part of its body. The darkness ran down the man's face, chest, and hands onto his merchandise, sliding over the surfaces like oil on top of water.

One of the girls in our group picked up a necklace. Despite the creature's darkness, the necklaces this man was selling were quite nice. Even so, she quickly set it back down, just as she would if she suddenly realized that it was covered with ants. The octopus-headed man told us all about how he made each necklace himself. As the group turned to continue on its way, he quickly handed a half-sheet of paper to the girl who had picked up the necklace. She thanked him the way you do when a stranger hands you something you don't really want and turned to rejoin the group.

The paper was a poorly made invitation to a "spiritual enlightenment" seminar. The cheap and oddly cut paper suggested that this seminar was decidedly low-rent. Judging by the octopus on our bearded friend's head, it was probably an invitation to some sort of cult.

I wondered, as we continued down the street, what all that dark ink on the necklaces was meant to do. It was obvious that the bearded man was thoroughly deceived, but could he really ooze deception onto anyone who had a taste for unique jewelry? Then I heard God ask me to look back.

I looked back and saw that the sky had been torn in half. A fissure of gold light cut across the sky above Venice Beach as if a giant knife had sliced open the wrapping on a golden, glowing gift. The tear in the sky followed the path we had taken along the beach. The light shone on everything within its reach. It was a bright and beautiful California summer day, but the rest of the world looked gray compared to anything that was touched by the brilliant light.

As the light engulfed the lady at the psychic booth, her tarnished, golden glasses caught the light and were renewed. Every dent and cut was repaired, and every jewel was shimmering as if it were new.

The black octopus demon slid away from the light, retreating from its bald perch to the shadows under the bearded man's jewelry table. The demons that had been weaving a macabre waltz across the sky shrunk away as if burned by the light, while the angels basked in its warmth.

The golden light followed in our wake for the rest of the day, cleaving the sky with its celestial glow. All we did was shop and occasionally release a silent prayer, but still the light followed. I knew the light wasn't permanent.

It was there because we were, and it would be gone soon after we left unless someone wanted it to stay.

The light restored the woman's gift, but it was her choices, wounds, or ignorance that had made it a tattered shadow of its original design. At least she had an opportunity to see what it could be. The bearded man had fallen into deception because he was coerced, either because the church hurt him or because he was just a lost man looking for something to touch his lonely heart. It doesn't really matter. He had an opportunity to look at the world without a lying voice filling his ear—a moment to see things clearly.

This didn't happen because my youth group was special. It didn't happen because we earned it through hours of intense prayer or biblical study. It happened because we asked. Our youth pastor had pulled us together for a short prayer session before we went shopping, where he asked that we would be a light, even on our recreation day.

You may be wondering why I didn't stop to talk to the psychic or why we didn't pray for the necklace salesman. Those were two out of the hundreds of people we walked by that day. All of them had a place that needed a touch from God, and all of them were affected by the light that followed us that day at Venice Beach. Part of me thinks that I missed a hundred opportunities to release more of God's love on that beach. The other part thinks that if I took every one of those opportunities, I'd still be down there. That's a balance I'm working on every day. But the light that followed us wasn't just something special that one time on that one day. When you're a child of God, you change everything you touch.

HOME

I'm at my house, doing my best to hide from a sweltering Georgia afternoon. My wife is out of town for the week, so the house has been in better shape. I'm in the rocking chair in our upstairs bedroom where there are a few too many pieces of laundry on the floor and about five half-full cups on my nightstand. I suppose it is better to build a collection of stacked glasses at my bedside than run the risk of having to go downstairs to fetch a glass of water.

There's a hole in the ceiling above my bed. Thankfully this hole doesn't exist in the physical world, because I am about as good at fixing things as I am at remembering that I already have a cup on my nightstand.

This hole is an "access point," a spot where the enemy can get in. Now, don't be silly; it's not like my walls are so thick or my front door so ingeniously locked that demons have to resort to clawing a small hole in my roof. Remember that when you see in the spirit, it is a visual representation of spiritual reality. That hole isn't really there, but it represents something that is.

I have been stressed about money lately because that's what happens when you're the male half of a young married couple with a new baby. That's probably why the hole is there. I know this because I feel the stress when I look at it. That's the interesting thing about demonic influence; it feels so real when you're in the middle of it, but the moment you see it clearly it's no more threatening than a papier-mâché bunny.

You affect the world around you, for better or worse. My worry about money has created an access point for the enemy to influence me. It's like carving a groove for water to flow.

This access point looks small. If it were physical, I probably couldn't even fit my hand through it. It looks like someone burned through my roof with a lighter or a small blowtorch. If I didn't change my thought patterns, my worries would continually dig at that hole, making it bigger. I've seen access points in people's homes that are coated in wax like a beehive or held open by black timbers like a mine shaft. This happens when demonic lies start mixing with worries or fears. It reinforces the enemy's access.

So I pray a simple prayer: "I command that access point to be closed up. I cover it with the blood of Jesus, and I repent for not trusting God to be my provider." Just like that, it heals itself. The angel over my baby's crib flies up to the spot and touches it with her hand. It glows for a moment, and that's that.

You don't need to copy my prayer. I don't use the same one every time, and half the time I don't pray at all. Not that there's anything wrong with praying protection over your house or anointing all the rooms with oil; these things are designed to be acts of faith. It's more important to change the way you think than to perform the correct ritual.

Your home is your environment. Your environment is a reflection of your habits and mind-sets. My wife is gone, so my environment is littered with dirty laundry and more cups than I'll likely need. It is a reflection of my disdain for cleaning up after myself. I could put the laundry in the hamper and carry all the half-full glasses downstairs in less than a minute, but my room will look like this again in few days if I don't change my habits.

I have been stressing about money, and that stress created an access point in my room. I have God-given authority I can use to shut any demonic door and chase any demon out of my house, but they can come right back in and build a new door if I don't change the habits and mind-sets that let them enter in the first place.

ART AND MEDIA

People often ask me if I can see spiritual entities in videos or photographs. The answer is no. I can't see a newscaster's guardian angel, and I can't tell if a talk show host has a demon on him. But I do see things come *out* of movies and television all the time. Most of it isn't all that surprising. Anointed worship music releases colorful lights and attracts angels. Heavy metal music can release anger. A frightening newscast may release fear.

Movies, TV shows, music, media, books, paintings, and video games—all of these things are created by people. And all of them carry a spiritual mark—good, bad, or somewhere in between.

Before you start cramming all your movies into the garbage disposal, remember that you are a child of God. All art carries spiritual weight, but your Dad is the Creator of the universe. Hiding from movies, throwing your TV out the window, burning all your books, and yelling at the kid playing a game at the back of church *can* be an act of fear. And you give power to the things you fear because fear is a kind of faith.

Fear is the expectation of attack or pain, meaning you

believe whatever you are afraid of has the capacity to do you harm. That belief is faith that darkness has power over you. It is a disservice to the authority God has given to you to be afraid of anything demonic.

Now, that doesn't mean you should go get a stack of the most violent movies you can find and watch them back-to-back in an attempt to prove your spiritual toughness. It just means that this is yet another area of life that requires the voice of the Holy Spirit.

The Crusades, the Spanish Inquisition, slavery, and the subjugation of women are just a few of the horrible things that have been done in the name of the Bible. Should you throw away your Bible? No. The point is that you need the voice of the Holy Spirit in your life for everything. Without it *anything* can be twisted, but with it *anything* can be redeemed. I was alone in my apartment one afternoon during the middle of my second year at Bethel School of Ministry, when I was also in the middle of the first iteration of this book. The process had been rocky to say the least. I have enjoyed writing from a very young age, but I always preferred writing fiction. Cataloging the events of my life in an interesting way was proving to be a much more difficult task than I expected. Frustrated, I popped on some headphones and began pacing the living room.

Scrolling through the music on my phone, a band I used to listen to in high school caught my eye. They were not a Christian group, and they had a penchant for punctuating their lyrics with profanity and extremist politics, which was against most of my personal values, but something about their honestly expressed frustration soothed my inability to put words on paper.

I continued to pace around my living room, listening to the band build into the first chorus. The lyrics were about social control and government conspiracy—topics that would turn up the noses of most good Christian folks, especially when communicated with wildly flanging guitar chords and angry lyrics shouted into a microphone. Despite this, I could not help but hear their words like the desperate cry in some of David's darker psalms.

The members of the band I was listening to didn't know they were calling for God to bring change to the social structure of their country, but God heard them anyway. And I could feel His heart responding.

All at once the world peeled away. One moment I was doing short laps around my living room, and the next I was standing in the middle of a flat desert. Though the spirit realm regularly appears before me as lucidly as anything in waking life, I rarely have a vision that overwrites my ability to see the physical world. In fact, this was only the second time I had found myself unable to see anything apart from what God was showing me.

I saw a woman standing in the center of the endless emptiness. She wore a long, flowing dress layered with fabrics in varying shades of blue and white. In her hand was a white staff. Darkness poured over the horizon— a black blanket spreading across the sun-bleached earth. The woman knelt and pressed her face to the cracked ground.

As the darkness drew closer, it became clear that it was not an indistinct mass but hundreds of thousands of demons of every size and shape. Giant, four-legged monstrosities were surrounded by dozens of smaller imps and ghouls. The air was rapidly filling with menacing winged creatures that further darkened the already cloudy sky.

The woman remained completely still as the sea of bloodshot eyes and gnashing teeth marched forward, covering the desert in undulating darkness.

Without warning, the throng came to a complete stop about fifty yards from her. A man with blue fire on his shoulders stood facing the dark army halfway between the demonic front and the woman wearing white and blue. I didn't know if he had just arrived or if he had been there the whole time. I'd been too focused on the woman to notice.

Though the vision completely blocked out my physical surroundings, the music from my phone was still pouring into my ears, more clearly than ever. The music came to a dramatic pause as the demonic army faced off with the man on fire.

The man charged toward the demonic horde just as the song kicked back into full overdrive. A ten-foot ape-like demon leaned forward from the crowd, drooling jaws agape, to consume the attacker. In a singular fluid movement of music and motion, the fire on the man's shoulders traveled down his right arm, congealed into a glistening blue sword, and cleaved the ape demon's jaw in two.

What followed was the most dramatic display of combat I had ever seen. Spinning and twirling faster than my eyes could follow, the man cut down demon after demon with impossible efficiency and speed. Even the dark-winged beasts that swooped down from the sky were sent tumbling along the dry ground, lifeless and bleeding. The demons fell by the hundreds, but still thousands more came, climbing over the growing mountain of bodies.

Step by step the man with the sword was pushed back until he was standing next to the kneeling woman. For the first time, the man turned to look at her. As if this had been what she was waiting for, the woman seized him by the hand, and all at once the tide turned.

Hand in hand, the woman with the staff and the man with the sword drove through the mass of demons like a chainsaw through tissue paper. What had been a desperate fight for the man alone was an elegant dance with the woman. Flashes of white and streaks of blue cut through the demonic army so furiously that I was periodically blinded.

The music in my ears and the battle before my eyes moved in flawless unison, a perfectly scored soundtrack to this glorious ballet of demonic destruction. Finally, the last demon fell. For the first time, the sun broke through the dark clouds. And then the song was over. My modest living room returned to view as the last few notes faded.

I didn't understand what I had seen or why I had seen it. My muscles were tense, and my heart was beating as if I'd just finished a marathon. I was beginning to calm down when the song started again. I only had a moment to wonder whether or not I had hit the repeat option before the vision came flooding back. The whole picture played across my eyes again, moment for moment and note for note. After it was done, I hit play once more to see if it would work. Again I saw the entire vision.

The band wrote songs of protest against a system that

they viewed as unjust and corrupt. I couldn't help but think that the vision was a representation of the truth that the only way the band could reach its seemingly insurmountable goal of social reform was through relationship with the Holy Spirit.

While the man with the sword's fight against the demonic onslaught had been valiant, it was no longer a fight once he partnered with the woman. It instantly gave me a new compassion and understanding for the members of the band, as well as a new view of my own insurmountable task.

∾

Unfortunately as Christians we tend to see everything that is *in* the world as being *of* the world. The truth is that people are complicated. They are not simply bad or simply good. Art carries the same spiritual complexity as its creators. I believe it is spiritually immature to say any creative work that doesn't perfectly comply with our belief system should be rejected or avoided. It would be equally immature to ignore our own personal convictions and just absorb everything.

The problem comes when we only look skin deep, both spiritually and physically. I could have looked at some of the spiritual activity that came from that band's style of music or the content of their song and decided that it was a hateful tirade of offensive angst. Yet still God's love was being drawn to the heart behind the music, much as Jesus was drawn to the tax collectors and prostitutes. This was not because He saw them as trash in need of treasure. It was because He saw them as treasure hidden beneath the trash.

When it comes to the things that enter through our eyes and ears, I believe that real maturity happens when we can learn to eat the meat and spit out the bones. Or, to put it in biblical terms, I think it happens when we separate the tares from the wheat. In this way we will not make the mistake of the Pharisees and be offended by Jesus when He comes in an unexpected way.

POWERS, PRINCIPALITIES, AND SO ON . . .

WHEN I WAS fourteen, my parents and I went to a prophetic conference in Jacksonville, Florida. We arrived late on the third night, walking in well after worship had started. The band was arranged in a broad arc, leaving a decent space in the middle of the stage where a giant lion was lying. It was basking in the glowing worship that emanated from the team and audience. It was easily three times larger than any lion you'd see on the African savanna, and the feeling of peace emanating from it was big enough to match.

After a few minutes of worship, I noticed a glass door on the left side of the stage with a green exit sign glowing above it. A man was standing just outside the door, and above him was the head of a massive black dragon peering into the building. Fear pulsed through my body as I looked at the dragon's face, which was easily as big as a sedan and lined with rows of horns. Instinctively I turned to the lion. With a lazy roll of its head, the lion looked at me, looked at the dragon, and then looked back at me.

With the resignation of a couch-sitting parent who has been asked to get a glass of water, the lion got up and walked toward the dragon. It must not have known the lion was coming, because the dragon's eyes remained fixed on the people in the room. The lion walked right underneath the black monster, gave a little hop, and tore a chunk out of the dragon's neck.

With a writhe of pain and blood pouring from its gaping wound, the dragon pulled its head back through the door. The lion made its way back to its spot on the stage, giving me one more reassuring look before it slumped back down to bask in the worship. This gave me the distinct impression that the only reason he had bothered to get up was to make me feel better.

Back at the door, the dragon was gone, along with the man who had accompanied it. After speaking with one of the conference organizers, I found out that several local occult leaders had threatened to curse the conference.

This is just one example, but the older I get, the more I realize that worrying about anything that doesn't worry God is a waste of time.

A principality, by my definition, is a demonic force with dominion over a specific geographic region. Sometimes they try to oppress an area with a specific negative trait, like financial ruin, perversion, or disunity; but this is not always the case. Demons, in most of my experience, are opportunists. They look for the cracks in our self-perception, attitude, and beliefs, then nuzzle into those cracks to try to make them worse. This is true on a personal level, but it is also true on a cultural level. I don't necessarily think that principalities inherently carry one particular bad trait; I think they look for what is wrong and try to make it worse.

I don't think that a particular area or country is full of poverty because a principality of poverty took dominion over them. In a situation like that, I would think that a culture of poverty began to develop, perhaps starting with just a few people or just a few unfortunate circumstances, a bad harvest, a fire, or a few failed business ventures. A principality, noticing an opportunity, could begin whispering lies into the ears of those who experienced loss because of those events. He would point to this situation and that situation, using evidence to slowly melt away people's hope. Soon people could begin to accept that "This is just how it is." Thus, that principality has helped perpetuate a culture where poverty is normal.

You may be thinking, "What's the difference? If a principality is there, then it's there. Why does it matter how it got there?" If a principality of poverty came barging into my city and caused economic disaster, then I am powerless to stop it apart from throwing prayers at it and hoping for the best. If, however, a principality snuck into my city and perpetuated an unhealthy mind-set that was already there, suddenly I am very powerful. Why? Because if he had to sneak in and slowly gain influence and authority, that means he didn't start with any; he had to steal it. And who do you think he stole it from?

∽

One day I was at the prayer chapel at Bethel Church in Redding, California. The prayer chapel is a separate building surrounded by a lovely walking garden at the top of a small hill. I was walking around said garden, when I felt compelled to stand next to the tree that overlooked the entrance to the Bethel campus. As I stood, minding my own business, a principality fell out of the sky and landed in front of me.

It had a long neck with a bulky body and thick tail. From head to tail, it was probably fifty yards. Its head had landed just at my feet, while the long neck and pale body stretched all the way down the hill.

I looked up and asked, "God?"

Immediately the creature began to writhe and shrivel, shrinking until it looked like a skinny, sallow person lying at my feet in the fetal position.

I heard it mumbling, "Don't kill me. Please don't kill me."

I looked up again. "What's this?"

God answered, "It is a principality of financial oppression."

"All right. So what do I do?"

"Rebuke him."

Without really thinking about what I was going to say, I looked at the disgraced demon and said, "You are not allowed to touch me or my family ever again."

It gritted its teeth in acknowledgment.

Since sniveling principalities don't make for very pleasant company, I turned and started back up the path toward my car. After a dozen steps, I heard a deep roar behind me. I turned to see the principality flexing and swelling to its original size as it stomped up the path after me. As it extended its neck, slobbering jaws open wide, a black streak fell from the sky. The principality's head shot from its neck as if it were spring loaded, sending it soaring past my left ear while the limp body tumbled by my right side.

I stood speechless, not particularly accustomed to

being charged down by principalities, much less one whose head spontaneously leapt from its body. A man was standing with his back to me at the spot where the principality had been decapitated. I only had a moment to observe the ornate sword in his hand before it dissolved into blue flames that ran up his arm, coming to rest across his shoulders. Just as I began to wonder who he was, the man turned around and I found myself staring back at me. Perhaps my standards for normality are different than most people's, but even for me this was very weird.

Then I heard God say, "You don't know the authority you have."

∼

I was in a service at Bethel one Sunday night. I was tired, so I had only planned to stay for worship. As soon as the music began to die down, I grabbed my coat and wove my way through the crowd. I managed to escape the building unhindered by friend or acquaintance but was stopped in the parking lot by something that was neither. As I approached my car, keys in hand, a beast appeared before me. It had the stocky, four-legged build of a bear or badger but the long snout of a wolf, and its muzzle was easily as big as my jeep.

We stood there a moment, staring at one another. He had beady yellow eyes and teeth too big for his drooling mouth.

I leaned to one side to see around his nose, since it seemed odd to address his nostrils. "Yes?" I said.

"Just looking," he replied.

"Then I guess I'll be going," I said, cutting a path around his bulky shoulder. By the time I'd reached my car, he'd gone.

I didn't put much thought into the exchange. By this time I had concluded that for the most part, it is a waste of time trying to figure out demons. Their tactics and words are laced with layers of deception so thick that pondering them is usually as pleasant and profitable as untangling knotted barbed wire. It always boils down to the same thing anyway: steal, kill, and destroy. Besides, God is quite excellent at revealing the plans of the enemy when necessary.

Several months passed before I saw the beast again. I was just arriving at Bethel on a cloudy Wednesday afternoon and was pulling into the gravel parking lot where I had seen the principality before. I locked my car door and turned toward the church, only to find a giant angel in my path.

He was easily ten feet tall and clad from head to toe in brilliant, golden armor. He had a thick neck and thick hands. I could spend a great deal of time describing the jewels that adorned every notch and accent of his heavy armor or the massive gold spear that looked like a stick in his hands but like a small tree to me. But what I remember most about him was his eyes.

I only had the courage to look for a moment, but in that moment a weight of glory sunk into my soul so deeply I still feel its heaviness. Those eyes had seen God, and I could feel God in them. The reflected glory was so frighteningly powerful that it made my encounter with the beast seem like meeting a puppy in the park.

When I hear God speak, I rarely hear words. Raw blocks of information land in my mind—sometimes feelings or entire lifetimes of thought—and my brain slowly unpacks them. This is how the angel spoke to me. I can translate these hunks of knowledge into English, but it often feels as though I am interpreting a poem without any of the rhythm or rhyme. The facts come through, but the weight of meaning in the original revelation is only partially retained. Perhaps this is just a limitation of human communication, or maybe it is simply because revelation is much better experienced than recited.

The angel turned away, but I knew I was meant to follow. I walked quickly; each of his steps required at least two of mine. We came to a bushy area behind the parking lot where a large tree trunk had fallen against a boulder. A tingling sense of fear began rising from the bottoms of my feet, up my legs, and into my chest. I would have run if I hadn't been two steps away from a ten-foot-tall angel with a burning spear.

I was about to ask the angel what I was feeling when I saw the source of the fear—a pair of glowing, yellow eyes, peering from under the log. In a flash the eyes came lunging out from the shadows, surrounded by a blur of black fur and gnashing teeth. The furious mass leapt into the air and then came to a choking halt inches from my face. A shriveled and sickly version of the beast that had blocked my path a few months before landed in a crumpled heap at my feet. As it lay there panting—much smaller than it had been, but still the size of a large dog—I noticed a golden chain clasped around its neck. The other end was wrapped around the stump of the fallen tree.

"What is it?" I asked the angel.

"A principality responsible for the destruction of students that leave the school of ministry."

After a few minutes of silence, I felt that I was free to leave if I wished. The angel followed me when I left.

"He is weak," the angel said as we walked, "and he knows that his time is short."

We didn't speak the rest of the way back. I gave the angel one last look before turning the key to unlock my car door. The tingling fear flooded my chest again, and a vicious, snarling shadow shot out from under my car. I watched as open jaws and dripping teeth came soaring at my shocked face for the second time that night.

From somewhere above me a burning spear was thrown and sunk deep into the beast's meaty back, pinning it to the ground. In a single motion the angel stepped in front of me, swung the spear in the air, and flung the principality back to the log where it had been chained.

For the second time that night I looked the angel straight in the eye. "He's not happy to lose his place," he told me, and then he was gone.

Principalities are, in my experience, violently territorial and aggressive toward those who challenge them. I've been around a fair number of people who feel the need to pray and intercede against these demonic entities, but this is something I've never had a strong inclination to do. Principalities, being demonic rulers over specific geographic regions, leave an open throne when they are brought down, and it seems to me that you shouldn't go tearing things off thrones that you aren't prepared to fill. Please don't think that I'm telling you to let these things just walk all over you or that I'm suggesting that you shouldn't pray. I'm simply asking you to think about what you pray.

It is human nature to focus on dealing with the symptom rather than the problem because the symptom takes less responsibility to correct. When we have a headache, we'd rather take a pill than drink six to eight glasses of water a day and reduce our sugar intake. We'd rather buy Diet Coke and fat-free sour cream than eat fruits and vegetables. And it's much easier to throw money at the needy than to develop a culture that prevents poverty.

Principalities can only stay where they have a place to land. While casting down a principality will remove it from its place, it is much more profitable and powerful to change the spiritual ecosystem that attracted it in the first place. If there is a spirit of poverty over your city, be generous. If there is a spirit of anger, release peace. If there is a spirit of homosexuality, release identity in Christ. If there is a spirit of fear, release love. That may seem like far too little when you're staring at the problems we all face, but that is just the point. Principalities strive to make us feel insignificant. Every single step we take, individually and corporately, toward a culture modeled after the kingdom of God is a victory. It is *possible* to cast down a principality through prayer, but it is *impossible* for a principality to remain in a culture that has made no room for it.

MY STORY

ACT TWO

THINGS WERE GOING nicely for me. I was going to a church that taught about growing in the gifts of the Spirit, and my parents and church leaders knew about the things I saw. Plus, it was nice to know that I wasn't stratospherically insane. All that I needed to do was learn how to put my gifts to good use.

I started off small. Our church had a weekly prophetic meeting where members of the team would spend thirty minutes prophesying over a new person each week. Unbeknownst to me, attending this meeting was the best thing I could have done for myself. Seeing in the spirit is all but worthless if you can't hear the voice of God.

I soon learned that there wasn't a great deal of difference between the prophetic and seeing in the spirit. Sometimes people would come with cuts and bruises on their faces. As each word was prophesied over them, liquid light would form in the air, repairing the cuts and clearing the bruises. Sometimes a member of the team would prophesy a new season of life, describing a vision of a blossoming tree. As the words were spoken, fresh grass and flowers would rise out of the carpet where the one receiving the word stood. It was hard to tell if these things were spoken because they were there in the spirit, or if they appeared in the spirit because they were spoken.

I learned a lot about the way God thought. I had known God for as long as I could remember, but this was the first time I'd *seen* what I'd known—His goodness made manifest in the lives of His people. It felt good to see eyes light up when I told them what their angels looked like. It was fun to describe what the Holy Spirit was doing when He caused people's hands to shake, and I never got tired of telling people what happened during worship.

It wasn't always easy, however. Seeing in the spirit came with unexpected responsibilities. Every angel I described drew a dozen questions, and every question I answered raised a dozen more.

Being an introverted, internal processor, I was put off by all the attention my gift attracted. People three times my age wanted to have dinner with me to talk about what I saw. I was regularly bombarded with deep philosophical questions about the nature of the universe. And a local professor even wanted me to visit his lab to run some tests on me. It was a lot for a thirteen-year-old to handle.

One of the prophetic leaders at the church took my mother and me under his wing. He didn't see the way that I did, but he was very gifted in the prophetic. I bounced the majority of what I saw off of him, and he did his best to discern what it meant and what I should do with it. I learned a great deal, but after several months some unfortunate things came to light. The leader, whom I had come to think of as a mentor, was found to be dealing with alcohol and homosexuality issues, along with some New Age tendencies. He was asked to resign his position at the church.

Learning all this about my mentor was like being roused from a daydream by a baseball bat. There was no doubt that he was a gifted man, but I didn't know where the lines between his divine gift and carnal limitations were, which caused me to question everything I had learned under his leadership. Lost and confused, I drew my gifts and myself inward.

I didn't know whom to talk with about the things that I saw, partially because the wound from my first confidant was still raw and partially because I was thirteen. With no place to share and new beings and visions appearing before me every day, I turned to the only person I knew who was sure to be familiar with the spirit realm—God.

It was much easier this way. I'd sit in the back of the church, watching angels carry glass jugs of different-colored oils into the rafters. They would stack them in long rows on the overhead beams and then wait patiently for some kind of signal.

When I would sit quietly and observe these kinds of actions while connecting with the presence of the Holy Spirit, simply watching would bring to mind the purpose. It was like an old familiarity being reawakened. I knew the angels were preparing for ministry time, and I knew they were excited. I expected them to take turns dive-bombing the crowd with their glowing payload, and when it happened, it seemed perfectly in place.

I guess that it would have felt the same if I learned to play football as a child, had been kept from seeing a game through adolescence, and then saw one again during adulthood. I probably wouldn't have been able to list the rules of the game or the roles of the players, but distant familiarity would bring out some of the meaning behind all the running and throwing. I believe that we are all made in the image of God. We are designed to understand Him and the way He speaks. Though many of the things I saw were new to me, I soon began to understand that God had given me everything I needed to make sense of the things I saw. I just had to be patient enough to let Him teach me.

Vision by vision I was building a spiritual vocabulary. I'd see a serpentine creature wrapped around someone's neck and know that they were allowing themselves to be controlled by a manipulative person. A tall angel with blond hair would pass me in the hall carrying a thick robe made of nighttime sky, and I'd know that someone was about to receive an impartation of wisdom. Lightning would strike a man in the front row during worship, sending him into a fit of convulsive laughter. I knew that this was God releasing His goodness. Most of what I saw made sense through osmosis. Understanding *what* everything was usually came with seeing it; understanding *why* it was there required dialogue with God.

Each year our church held a weekend-long worship conference. Fortunately we had an abundance of talented worship leaders, so filling all seventy-two hours of continuous worship wasn't too difficult. The majority of the experienced leaders picked up the slots during the day, while the less confident worship leaders and youth bands took the twilight hours. Since my parents were on staff, I spent a good deal of the weekend in the worship room. I'd decided to stay until midnight the first night because a friend of mine was leading from eleven thirty to one.

I took up my typical post at the back wall of the sanctuary watching a half dozen or so angels casually drift around the three people who made up the audience. The mellow tones drifting from the frets of my friend's beat-up guitar were congealing into a white fog that was being pushed around by the angels' circular flight pattern. It was nothing overly dramatic or interesting, but just the kind of relaxed mood you want as the clock nears midnight.

For no reason in particular I decided to watch as the minute hand met the hour hand at the apex of the clock on the back wall. Just as the clock struck twelve, I was flung against said wall.

I'd never been one to experience the physical manifestation of God's presence regularly. Not that I had never shaken or fallen down under the influence of the Spirit, but it just wasn't something that happened often. However, the moment Friday turned to Saturday during this docile worship session, I found myself powerless against this unexpected weight of glory.

It felt as though the entire room had just shot forward and up at three thousand miles per hour—the velocity pinning me to the back wall. The sensation continued for a few seconds, and then the ceiling began to break off. The top of the building broke apart as if it were being peeled open by a hurricane, and clouds rushed past as the wall behind the stage began to buckle.

Though I felt a moment away from being blown out the side of the building, the musicians on stage continued to play mildly. The clouds rushed past faster and faster. At first they were as dark as the night sky, but as we climbed higher, they began to reflect golden light. Though most of my attention was on keeping my fingernails dug into the drywall, I couldn't help but be drawn to look at the distant, encroaching light.

The light became painful to look upon, reflecting on every cloud from every direction, blinding. As quickly as it started moving, the room came to a complete halt. I braced myself, expecting to be flung forward as I would if a speeding car came to a sudden stop. Instead I slumped to the floor.

After regaining the capacity to distinguish up from down, I pulled both feet underneath myself and stood up. The room, now only consisting of a floor and the wall I had been leaning against, had come to rest at the perimeter of a vast, golden city. Giant drifts of sparkling cloud, ignited by some unseen light source, swam through the mile-high buildings, giving them an otherworldly sheen.

The architecture was like none I'd ever seen. Each building looked like a completely different visionary had designed it, though none looked like it didn't belong with the others. I probably stood gazing at the city for a total of ten seconds, which is a very long time to stare at something incomprehensibly beautiful. The band continued to pluck out its simple melody, apparently oblivious to the wonder just behind them—yet somehow still perfectly a part of it.

A sudden yank and the church sanctuary was falling back to planet Earth much faster than it had ascended. The descent took less than a second, but it was more than enough time to notice the completely weightless sensation in my stomach and listen to the gentle whisper that God spoke in the quiet of my heart: "I can't help but draw them close to Me."

God always had a way of expressing a lifetime of love in a few simple words. It was less about what He said than how He said it, and less about how He said it than the feeling that burned in my heart when He did. Everything

I saw—every single thing—was a completely fresh glance at the same all-consuming love.

I understood when I saw a light come from heaven and gently wrap its way around a woman with a heart tied up in barbed wire that His affection was making it new, but my mind could only grasp a small portion of the magnitude of love happening before me. The nuance with which the light navigated every infected twist and turn of the fleshy mess suggested a tenderness that mere words could not describe. At least I could understand why we would be spending an eternity admiring His goodness. It would take that long to comprehend the kindness of even His lightest touch.

At that time I knew the things I saw were more significant than my young mind could understand. This more than anything was what compelled me to start sharing my visions again. It continued to be frustrating, however. People were so entranced by the most mundane parts of the spirit realm.

Yes, there's an angel over there, cleaving the head off every demon that comes within fifty feet. But what about the way God's hand is on that worship leader? How can a simple touch communicate so much affection?

I suppose it was natural. An angel performing wholesale demonic massacre is a lot more viscerally interesting than God touching someone. Still, I couldn't escape the feeling that I was failing to communicate the depth of meaning behind what I was seeing.

The things I saw were often abstract, both in meaning and appearance. But the understanding that came when I saw in the spirit felt both natural and simple in my mind. Trying to explain this meaning to others, however, was like describing water to someone who had spent his or her entire life on the moon.

Other prophetic and church leaders attempted to mentor me. Admittedly I never fully let any of them in. They encouraged me to share the things I saw, and I'd get frustrated at the deluge of attention and unanswerable questions that poured in after every shared encounter. With each attempt I grew more hesitant.

Seeing this hesitancy as something to overcome, the leaders would continue to encourage me to speak. But since each try resulted in no tangible improvement, I began to take their enthusiasm as unwanted pressure.

Looking back, I think the real frustration was that no one knew what to do for me, and I had no idea what I needed from anyone, anyway. Disillusioned and frustrated, I once again slowly stopped talking about seeing in the spirit altogether.

First, I stopped sharing the bad things I saw, which was easy because that rarely got any kind of good reaction. Then I stopped answering the questions people asked. This didn't make very many people happy, but it was easier to deal with disappointment than the endless, impossible questions.

Before long, the only time I shared the things I saw was when God told me to. He usually had to ask me two or three times, and after I'd stretched the line of disobedience as far as it would go, I'd simply whisper the things I'd seen in the pastor's ear and reject his offer to share what I saw on stage.

Despite my near complete silence on the subject, I continued to see more and more every day, and God continued to talk with me about the things that I saw. It was comforting. I could be the one who asked the questions, and He always had the answers—or at least a kind way of saying that I would need to wait to understand.

I made my way through junior high and high school being as normal as I could, only addressing my so-called gifting when it would be direct disobedience to do otherwise. I thought that it would stay this way forever. Little did I know that God had other plans for me.

PART II

ANGELS AND INFINITY

WAS AT A party earlier today. I don't really like parties, so I was sitting on a couch, doing my best to look as if I were enjoying myself and passing the time by observing my fellow attendees.

Situations like these can get complicated. There were about three dozen people mingling with each other, each with a personal angel. Each of those angels was interceding for, protecting, or otherwise blessing his or her person in his or her own unique fashion. Some were dancing around the room and worshipping; others were massaging the shoulders of their people, whispering words of encouragement in their ears; while some simply stood, patiently listening to the myriad layers of conversation.

Each person in the room was surrounded by what I call a spiritual ecosystem. These are usually a combination of giftings, thoughts, and God's presence—the spiritual surroundings that are cultivated by physical and mental life.

Some of the people looked as if they were cloaked in a thick blanket of warm light, crowns on their heads and swords in their hands. One guy I knew on the far side of the room was covered head to toe in dense green foliage, with a ring of flowing water swirling around his head. It seemed strange until I remembered that he spent hours playing worship music on his guitar alone in his room. That kind of worship always attracts life.

The air was buzzing with thoughts. Insecurities darted

through the air like shadowy mice looking for a hole to hide in. The general buzz of excitement and joy was hovering over the crowd like calm, slow-motion fireworks. I could see a few scattered worries hanging over a few people's heads—swelling dollar bill signs and abstract images of unfamiliar relatives, each representing the telltale signs of money woes and family trouble, respectively. A girl was wandering through the crowd with a giant, smoky heart following close behind, every ignored glance and awkward greeting twisting its form.

There were a fair number of demons weaving their way through the crowd—about six, which is pretty normal for a crowd of this size. They snatched at the insecure thoughts, trying to get a grip on the fears that would otherwise be easily overcome or ignored. One had latched itself onto a middle-aged man's back, digging into the bald part of his head with long clawed fingers. It was probably trying to increase the discomfort he must have felt from being in a group of mostly younger people.

As you can see, it doesn't take much for this to get very complicated—not to mention crowded. Add in the angels that were just hanging around the room unattached to anyone in particular, the liquid-gold presence of God that was sweeping through the room in time with the music, the prophetic words falling from heaven for the people in the room, and all the various blessings and curses floating through people's conversations, and you can imagine how aimless this would be without the Holy Spirit as a guide.

I used to be overwhelmed when I'd see this much at once. I was barely able to keep it sorted in my brain, hardly having room to consider how to respond. Over the years I've become much more adept at letting the teeming spiritual sprawl fade into the background so that I can look to where the Holy Spirit is pointing me.

I was immediately drawn to the man on my left. I knew him well enough to ask why he was worried about money, and he knew me well enough to know that I was seeing it swirl around his head.

We had a short conversation that, quite honestly, didn't entirely dispel his worries, but at least I was able to encourage him. As we spoke, I saw a golden package tied with bright red ribbon float through the sky. It landed gently on the top of his head and remained there for as long as I saw him that day. I had the impression it was waiting for him to reach up and open it.

The words we speak in the physical realm move mountains and bend destinies in the spirit realm. Here, you encourage someone; there, you give the tools to climb out of a pit. Here, you lay your hand on someone's shoulder; there, you're marking a life for blessing. Here, you say a simple prayer; there, the hosts of heaven receive their battle commands. Here, you sing a pretty song; there, you stand in the throne room of God, releasing glory to the King of all kings. Here, you drop a check in an offering bin; there, you set your crown at His feet. On Earth you pray for a sick person; in heaven you are a coheir with Christ, pouring the bounty of His kingdom onto His children.

PEOPLE

SEEING A PERSON in the spirit is a lot like getting to know his or her personality. You see a few facets and layers and think that you know this person pretty well, but then you peel back another layer and another, often discovering that you knew nothing at all.

Once a friend and I traveled from Northern California to her parents' house in Washington to attend the wedding of a mutual friend. Once there, she stood in the kitchen talking with her sister and mother, while I sat on the couch watching TV with her brothers, doing my best not to act as awkward as I felt.

I'd known my friend for a good three months at this point, and I thought I knew her well. She talked about her family constantly while we were at school—about all the fun they had growing up and how hard it was to live so far away. All of those talks made sense when I saw the way she smiled when she was with them. Our eyes met for a moment, probably because she was checking on me, and at that second the world melted away.

Sparkles dotted her pupils. I looked closer and was sucked straight into them. What had looked like sparkles from across the room were now images, twinkling and swirling around me, as I stood stunned.

A picture of athletes running in the Olympics flashed by me, just as a brown-haired girl broke across the finish line. Another picture of the same brown-haired girl caring for a patient in what looked like a doctor's office came swimming from somewhere behind me. I saw her again, running down the aisle in a white dress—a tuxedoed man with a hidden face waiting for her at the front. It was then that I realized that I was seeing dreams. Children, Christmases, birthday parties, and the warm smiles of a hundred people I'd never met rushed around me in every direction.

Then the dreams became memories. I watched a mom comforting a child with a scraped knee, friends laughing at a joke that the brown-haired girl had made, and parents getting mad at a messy room. The memories flew by faster and faster. They came so quickly I hardly saw what most of them were, but I felt every single one. Good, bad, embarrassing, scary, victorious, elating, painful, sad, and joyful—a solid stream of memories poured across my vision.

I felt uneasy at first, like someone who had just stumbled into the middle of an obviously private conversation. But that disquiet faded as a love began to burn in me. It wasn't the giggly flutter that runs through your stomach when you're sixteen and see a pretty girl, but rather a pure and honest adoration. It was a love that required nothing. I didn't need to be closer to her. I didn't need her to love me back. I didn't need her to accomplish anything great. I didn't need her to ever speak to me again. The love was complete from beginning to end, just as it was.

I fell back into the living room with a snap. It felt as if I'd been watching dreams and memories for hours, but now that I was back, I realized that not a moment had passed. As I looked at the real brown-haired girl who stood in the kitchen laughing with her mother, the feeling of love only grew stronger.

I didn't just see her as a person. I saw her as the perfect sum of every moment and memory that had led to this day, as well as the complete fulfillment of every single dream that lay hidden behind her eyes. I imagined that this must be how parents feel when they see their daughter at her graduation or their son on his wedding day. That's when I knew that I was seeing her as God did.

One year later I asked her to marry me, and every day from then until now has been a testament of just how good one decision can be. Sure, we argue. We have bad days. I say stupid things. But no matter what, whether my feelings are hurt or I'm mad at something she said, I can't help but remember the day I learned how much God loves her.

It sounds nice and easy when I put it that way. The fact is that I can't always see April for who she is. The fact is that even though I saw her for who she was that day in her parents' kitchen, it took a yearlong process of communication, hurt, joy, pain, and hours of talking before we were ready to be married. I saw everything I needed in a moment, but I will spend the rest of my life working out the truth of that revelation.

People sometimes tell me that they're afraid to pursue seeing in the spirit because they think seeing the demonic will overwhelm them. The truth is that it's much more terrifying to see how much God cares for us, as I did with April that day. God's love is a love that changes everything it touches. You can never go back once you've seen it. You'll forgive when you don't want to, give up anger before you're ready, and become friends with people you wouldn't have wanted to even sit next to before—all of it inspired by the profound revelation of His unyielding love.

∽

People are difficult to describe. This is just as true in daily life as it is in the spirit. We are complicated, insecure, untrusting, wounded, broken, petty, pretentious, weak, proud, crass, raw, apathetic, cowardly, hopeful, deep, excitable, bold, creative, beautiful, unique, profound, wise, hilarious, happy, and still somehow made in the image of God.

For example, I'm sitting outside of a cafe, surrounded by the cloudy chill of a September afternoon. My food is taking a bit longer than I'd like, so I distract myself by watching two men who are sitting at the table to my right, each probably somewhere in his late fifties.

They each have Bluetooth headsets, polo shirts, and leather shoes. Notebooks and papers cover the majority of their table. I can hear their conversation well enough to know that they're talking business—one trying to sell the other on some idea. I'll call man number one Hank, and man number two George.

Hank looks a touch older. His hair is grayer, and his shoes are slightly more out of style. I'm guessing that Hank is trying to decide whether he is going to buy what George is selling because Hank has a lot of thoughts bouncing around his head. A set of scales are floating behind him, weighing and measuring chunks of green rock and raw gold. He's trying to figure out if this deal is going to be good for him, just as anyone would, but that's not all he has on his mind.

I keep seeing a picture of a young man fall into the mix, and the moment I see him I know it's Hank's son. It's obvious from the sporadic way that the picture keeps popping up that Hank is worried about his son and that this deal will somehow affect him as well.

Hank is a good man, but you don't need to see in the spirit to know that. Deep grooves under his eyes and cheeks mark a face made for smiling, while his posture and voice both speak of an enduringly good nature. His hands glow a soft orange. Seeing it makes me understand that this is a man of compassion and generosity.

On his back is a net filled with toys, money, sports equipment, mobile phones, turkey dinners, and time. This is a man who likes to give gifts to his family and considers anyone within reach *family*.

George, the other man at the table, has sharp features and a crisp voice. He is sitting with his head jutted forward. A demon is sitting on his right shoulder—a small and sly bat-like figure. Its hand is sunk into the skin of George's left shoulder.

A heavy perfume of sweet words and vague promises is pouring from George's mouth. It looks like a flow of smoke that has been dyed and dressed up to look and taste like fresh air. He is clearly trying to get Hank to buy into whatever he is selling while trying to conceal some of the less positive facts at the same time.

At second glance, however, I notice that net full of gifts around Hank's neck looks heavy—strained cords strapped around strained shoulders. I imagine that Hank takes on too much responsibility for others and doesn't know how to give his burdens to God. A black iron clasp is digging deep into his right wrist with a chain stretching from the clasp to the wallet in his back pocket. He is probably overcommitted to work and feels guilty about the strain this puts on his family. The enemy is trying to turn his generosity into a trap. After seeing this, I realize the lines on Hank's face seem more like lines of stress than the result of a lifetime of smiling.

I look past George's tough and pointed demeanor, catching his eye for a brief moment. In that split second I see why the demon has such a comfortable place on his shoulder. I see George's father, a wealthy business owner, standing over him. George was asking his father to invest in a business idea.

The father rested his hand on George's left shoulder and whispered, "If I had to crawl from the bottom, then so do you." He smiled as he lifted his hand, unable to see the hole that his words had burned into George's shoulder.

Then I see the day the demon came. The hole was almost the perfect size for its spindly hand. Looking now, I can see that the wound has healed, sealing the demon's hand inside. After realizing this, when I look again at the words coming from George's mouth, it doesn't look as if he's trying to hide the facts to wring money out of Hank. Instead it looks as if he's afraid that Hank won't go for his idea, and the only way he's ever learned to deal with fear is through manipulation. Now I can see that George is a brilliant man. He has an eye for creating plans that benefit all parties involved. His angel is standing behind him with armfuls of blueprints and business plans all written in gold ink.

People are difficult to describe. This is just what I saw about Hank and George over the last few minutes. I can see what God made them to be, and I can see what hurt and lies have turned them into. Who are they, then? I imagine that some days they are what God made them to be and some days they are the product of pain and disappointment. But most of the time they are probably a little of both.

It's our job to bring out the best in everyone around us by expecting the best from them, by giving the benefit of the doubt, and by constantly looking for ways to encourage. Because if seeing in the spirit has taught me anything, it's that there's enough good in this world to take up 100 percent of your attention and enough bad to take up 100 percent of it as well.

∾

I used to work in the meat department at a certain warehouse store on the north side of Atlanta. I was cleaning up one Friday evening, keeping one eye on the clock as it approached closing time. Since I finished early, I decided to take my time cleaning the large windows that looked out on the store floor. The rest of my fellow workers had already left, which I was happy about because I find that it's easiest to think when I'm working and no one else is around.

As I cleaned the windows, I started looking at all the people walking around the store. I've never met anyone who didn't have a personal angel, and there wasn't a single exception walking in front of the meat department.

"How can every person in the world have a personal angel?" I wondered as I watched the waves of Friday night shoppers pick up their New York strips and chuck roasts. Right now there are 7,521,290,035 people on this planet—with a little more than four being born and a little less than two dying each second.[1] That's a lot of angels for a lot of people!

As I thought about the immensity of the inflating ter-restrial population, a man came in front of the window and started looking at the steaks. He was wearing a nice sweater that matched his nice jeans and complemented his nice shoes. He had clean, dark skin, close-cropped hair, and a kindly confident posture—altogether put together.

His angel was about a foot taller than he was with a thin and gently masculine face. He paid me no mind as he stayed by his person's side. He wore a pale-blue cloak that looked like it had been made for traveling.

"What happens when their person dies?" I wondered. "Do they just look for someone else? Are they assigned?"

The angel with the well-dressed man looked up as if I had said my thoughts out loud. As soon as our eyes met, I was pulled into a vision. I knew that I was standing in the meat department and still had a sense of my sur-roundings, but all my attention was pulled toward the vivid images that ran through my head.

I saw a young black woman giving birth—the angel with the blue cloak standing by her side. It was a per-fect baby girl, and the angel looked as enthralled as the mother. I watched the girl grow up. I saw a Christmas when her mother couldn't afford to buy the dolls the girl wanted but instead gave her some secondhand toys from the thrift store. I watched as her father shouted and drank his way in and out of her life. The angel was always there to hold her when tears poured from her eyes and hide her when her father's anger turned physical.

I saw the angel comfort her when the kids at school made fun of her clothes and teach her when there was no one there to help with her homework. I watched him laugh when she first learned to ride a bike and weep the first time she used drugs to numb the wounds her father gave her.

The angel was with her when she left home in rage, swearing to never come back, and he stayed with her the first time she sold her virtue to keep from starving. Years of brokenness and pain wore away most of the little girl left in her face, but still the angel followed her, caring for the woman the way he cared for the child.

I saw a dark alley drenched in nighttime rain and a man with darkness in his heart taking what dignity she had left by force. The angel stood over her, a sword in each hand, fighting off the encroaching darkness with absolute fury. I've never seen anyone fight so hard for anything. Still the darkness closed in, leaving the woman with bruises on her neck where defiling hands had squeezed out her last breath. The angel fell to his knees, and the image faded.

Next I saw another mother giving birth. This time the angel with the blue cloak smiled down at a baby boy. I watched him grow up with piles of presents at Christmas given by roomfuls of uncles, aunts, and grandparents who all knew how to love. The angel helped push the boy on his first bike alongside the boy's father. I watched his parents provide for the boy's every need. They weren't wealthy, but they weren't wanting.

The angel stood by the boy's side while his father taught him about business and finances. He cheered at graduations, shouted at football games, and laughed at awkward school dances—always accompanied by parents with smiling faces. I watched as the boy grew into the young man who stood in front of me, picking out steaks for dinner.

Then I saw another picture. The young man was driving through the streets of downtown Atlanta on a dark and rainy night. The blue-cloaked angel rode in the passenger seat. As the well-dressed man came to a stoplight, the angel reached out a hand and pressed it against the man's chest. The car came to a slow stop, even though the light was green. With his other hand the angel pointed out the passenger window at a dark alley.

Hesitance written all across his face, the man got out of his car and walked down the alley. The angel followed. There the man found a dead prostitute next to a Dumpster. The angel in the blue cloak knelt, weeping over the girl, while the same angel also walked by the well-dressed man's side. The kneeling angel stood, made eye contact with himself, and then vanished so that only he remained with the man.

The hesitant expression still hanging on his face, the man leaned over the dead woman and laid his hand over her heart. Immediately the empty lungs filled and the girl arched her back as life came rushing back to her. The man helped her to her feet and then to his car. They drove off in the pouring rain—the angel riding in the backseat.

I wiped the tears from my face and looked at the blue-cloaked angel who stood on the other side of the meat department window.

"Did that already happen?" I thought.

The angel shook his head.

I understood his meaning. "Then, will it happen like that?" I asked in my mind. "Will he save her?"

The angel looked down and gave a resigned smile. I saw the answer on his face more clearly than if he had said it out loud: "He could."

ANGELS

A NGELS ADORN THE stained-glass windows and ceilings of twelfth-century cathedrals, are the subjects of numerous books, and even had their own television program in the nineties. They have been an object of fascination and debate throughout Christian history. While I have a problem with people becoming so fascinated with the angelic that they forget to pursue a relationship with their Creator, I've come to think that learning about angels is almost impossible to do without also learning about God's nature.

In this section I will outline a few of the kinds of angels I have encountered over the years. Though many of them are different in appearance and demeanor, I don't believe that they are different kinds of beings. Instead, I think that they are all the same "species," each with unique roles.

A strong-shouldered construction worker in a hard hat looks fairly different from a skinny computer programmer who hardly sees the sun, yet both are human. Thinking of angels this way makes the differences in appearance and demeanor seem less odd.

While the next few sections are in no way an exhaustive list of all the types of angels, it is a good snapshot of the various roles that God's celestial servants play.

PROTECTION ANGELS

After discovering that my visions were not the result of a dangerous chemical imbalance, I quickly began taking every opportunity to learn about the things I saw. And protection angels were some of the first spiritual beings that I saw with any real understanding.

I used to perch myself near the back of the church so that I could get a broad view of what was happening in the spirit realm during the services. For a few months the majority of what I saw was no more discernible than an internal combustion engine would be to a caveman. I saw a lot of movement, and I had the distinct impression that all of it had a very precise order and rhythm that my inescapably human brain simply couldn't grasp.

Then one Sunday morning during worship, I noticed an elderly looking angel standing in front of the door to the foyer. His white-haired head was held high with an expression that was more regal than pompous, though it took a second glance to be sure. He wore shining silver armor that gave me a Greco-Roman impression. A long sword with an ornate silver handle sat at his hip. A small brass horn hung on the opposite side.

I was fascinated because for the first time I could remember, the more I looked at this angel, the more detail I could see. In the past, any angel or demon I saw appeared either as an indistinct blurb of shadow and light or an unchanging, clear image. This angel became clearer and clearer as I looked at him. I was at least a tennis court away from where the angel stood, but I could see the etching in his sword and the facets of his armor as clearly as if they were within reach. Letters were carved into the sides of the horn, though they were written in a language I'd never seen.

As I noticed these details, I understood each one. I knew the etchings on his sword and armor were a badge of long and devoted service. I knew the words written on the horn at his side were a declaration that could break down any wall (looking at them brought the story of Jericho to mind). And I knew each line in the angel's strong and aged face was a mark of his earnest commitment to his perpetual vigil.

In seeing these things, I began to understand protection angels. They were not so much physical protectors as they were a symbol of the all-encompassing protection of God, like the honor guard a king would send with a trusted ambassador.

It is one thing for a leader to employ a large army of powerful soldiers; it is another thing for a leader to inspire the unflinching devotion that I saw in the lines of that angel's face. Seeing him revealed his identity as well as the nature of his creator.

WORSHIP ANGELS

There was a period in my life when worship was an extremely frustrating experience. Being a fifteen-year-old boy probably had a lot to do with it, but at the time I attributed this dissatisfaction to the 780 or so Sunday morning worship services I had attended in my brief life.

The church my family and I attended had the best group of musicians and singers of any place we'd been, a committed and talented worship pastor, and a senior pastor with an immensely strong value for worship. Regardless, I couldn't seem to bring myself to care.

I talked with God more than anyone else, but I couldn't worship Him on a Sunday morning without a sour taste forming on the back of my tongue. And I did my best to blame everyone else for this problem.

I made excuse after excuse: That earthy lady twirling her flamboyant flags at ninety miles an hour is too distracting. This style of music is just not my thing. The worship team must not care that much about God, if they all run out for coffee the minute they step off the stage. Half these dancing people are just drifting with the flow of general enthusiasm; they don't know what they're dancing for.

I even began using my seeing gift to stock up on ammunition: How can I worship when this guy next to me keeps undressing the backup singer with his eyes? Why should I care what the worship leader is singing about if all he can think about is his marital problems? It's too hard to focus on God when the drummer is constantly worrying about looking good on stage.

Then I saw a worship angel.

I had seen angels worshipping before. The colorful and often abstract beings adorned the stages and rode on the words of every church body during every single one of those 780 services I'd had the fortune to attend. The beauty and grace with which they expressed their devotion to God was always a source of great enjoyment and encouragement, but until that day, however, I had never truly seen a worship angel.

This angel looked young. Angels exist outside of time and are therefore without age, but she looked no older than sixteen. Two brightly lit angels danced in the air above her, twirling and twisting in a way that left several trails of iridescent light. She wore a plain robe—it was the same off-white color you would paint the waiting room in a dentist's office—and had her hair drawn back in a simple ponytail.

She sat on her knees with her face pressed into the carpet, and her arms extended outward, palms flat on the floor. Every few seconds she would lift her face from the carpet and gaze toward the ceiling. Tears poured down her cheeks, more in waves than droplets. Her arms reached to the heavens, stretching out desperately while still maintaining a posture of thankfulness.

The look on her face caused my heart to skip a beat. Painful depths of longing were being answered by waves of fulfillment so complete that the satisfaction and joy were more tangible than the ground under my feet. This cycle of yearning and gratification continued, back and forth, faster and faster, until I could hardly bear to watch it. The angel must have felt the same, because just as I felt my heart was about to burst, she resumed her facedown position on the carpet.

The action she performed may seem simple when described in plain text. This is because I find it impossible to express the level of heart that was put into that simple act of worship. Still, even as I write about it now, I find my hands start to shake and my heart begins to burn.

Overwhelmed and ashamed, I turned away from the angel. The purity of her passion made the apathy of my heart feel suddenly pathetic and petty. Looking back at the show-off drummer, I couldn't help but see his desire to do well in his worship to God. The dangerously twirling flag woman looked more like a child overwhelmed with joy than an attention-starved spinster. Even the man who kept glaring at the backup singer had a heart that was visibly smoldering with hunger for an encounter with God's heart.

It didn't take long for me to realize that I was seeing worship the way God did. No insecurity, selfishness, or sin was powerful enough to hide His children from His affections. His love instantly overcame it all.

He never reprimanded me for having a bad attitude, and He never asked me to change. However, seeing His love for His people made it impossible for me to ignore the goodness that He put in each one of them. It made me sad that I had let such trivial issues sabotage my desire to express my love to Him. He certainly wasn't letting their quirks and inadequacies hamper His ability to receive their love.

PERSONAL ANGELS

Personal angels do, in fact, guard you during your daily comings and goings, but I don't like it when people call them guardian angels. To consider them a kind of one-man personal secret service is a tragic oversimplification. A personal angel is more like a resourceful personal assistant than a muscle-bound bouncer. I've never met anyone with more than one, and I've never met anyone without one.

You can learn a lot about someone by looking at his or her personal angel. A sick and sad angel is usually paired with a person who doesn't spend any time in God's presence. A sunny and bouncy angel is often accompanied by a cheery girl with a deep passion for worship, while a dignified and precisely dressed angel might be partnered with the CEO of a major corporation. Then again, sometimes the elated dancing angel is paired with the CEO, while the prim and proper angel is doing its best to look dignified while the cheery worship girl is dancing and twirling around the room. Whether by being opposites or complementary, personal angels always add a divine accent to their people.

Maybe it's just because they hang out with people more often than other angels, but personal angels seem to have a lot more personality than others. Perhaps they've spent so much time in the day-to-day happenings of the human stage play that all the parts have become familiar.

They smile with matriarchal satisfaction at the teenager who is stumbling his way through a conversation with a pretty girl. They watch with concern as we fight our way through difficult choices. They embrace us with brotherly love when storms of responsibility threaten to surge forth and devour us whole.

Personal angels, much like parents, see us at our best, at our worst, when we're young, when we're old, when we're smart, and when we're dumb. It is encouraging that despite all this, they still find us to be worth their company.

∽

I've been doing my best to write in a wide variety of locations looking for interesting things to share with my intrepid readers. It turns out, however, there aren't many public places where you can sit with a laptop for several hours, occasionally staring at strangers, without attracting odd looks. So here I am back at another coffee shop.

There's another laptop girl sitting at the table directly across from mine—headphones in ear, notepad on lap. Her angel, sitting in the chair next to her, has blonde hair, blue eyes, and a sunny complexion. I'd say about 30 percent of personal angels look like the person they are with, and this is one of those cases. The angel is peering from the girl to the laptop screen and back again in the longing way a puppy might look at a bouncy ball that's just out of reach. She notices that I'm looking at her—the angel, that is—and stands up.

She's wearing what could be described as robes, but their layered, multitone style makes them look fairly different from what you probably think of when I say "robes." She's a lot taller than she looked when she was sitting—at least a foot taller than me.

The angel looks down at her person, running her fingers through the blonde hair that so closely resembles her own. When she was sitting, the angel looked somewhere around nineteen. Now that she's standing, however, she's taken on an older, more motherly appearance.

Things are beginning to become clear. I see pictures of long nights spent studying matched against long days working and attending classes. Looking at the girl, who couldn't be older than twenty-one, I feel a sense of maternal longing. This is a girl who needs a mom, but she also needs to have more fun.

The blonde angel appeared young and looked longingly at her person because the angel was a representation of the girl's need for fun and rest. The angel then appeared motherly because the girl is probably missing the nurturing and comforting touch of a mother in her life.

It's important to remember that angels are spiritual

beings; they are not limited by a physical body the way people are, and they don't exist in time the same way that we do.

I was with a group of friends one day, and one of them could see in the spirit very much as I do. A girl in the group asked us to describe what her angel looked like. I looked and saw that it was a tall and slender man wearing wispy, white robes and a solemn but peaceful expression on his thin face. Before I said what I saw, the friend who sees in the spirit said that the angel looked like a fat pink lady bouncing around the room.

God answered before I could ask the question, "My creation reflects Me, and I have many facets." Immediately I understood.

If you met me on a day when I was tired or had a lot on my mind, you'd probably think that I was a quiet and contemplative person. If you met me on a day when I was with a group of my closest friends and having a good time, you'd probably think I was a boisterous, humorous, and charming person. Both descriptions are accurate, and both are part of who I am. Angels, not being limited by physical form, show these kinds of personality traits in their appearance. I was seeing the serious and peaceful aspect of that angel's personality while my friend was seeing the fun and joyful side.

ACTIVATION ANGELS

I lived in a bad part of town during my third year at the school of ministry. This was because I had almost no money. I felt, even at the time, that it was the perfect bachelor experience before my upcoming marriage.

The crappy apartment, messy roommates, endless supply of junk food, and regular all-night video game sessions were the ideal contrast to the new life I would be entering via the bonds of holy matrimony. And I planned to enjoy it while it lasted. After all, it was preferable to letting the situation drive me completely insane.

One particular night I was on my way back from a convenience store that was situated just a few dozen yards from our apartment building. I wouldn't likely be mistaken for a body builder or boxing champion, but I am over six feet of reasonably built masculinity that could at least send a fist in the general direction of an assailant, if necessary. Still, I was happy to be getting home before the sun fully set.

I was well into a bag of sour cream and cheddar chips, which had been surprisingly difficult to eat without dropping the rest of my shopping bags, when I arrived at my front door. I paused with my hand on the doorknob, feeling a presence arrive behind me.

These unexpected visits had recently become a more regular occurrence, so I wasn't surprised to find an angel when I turned around. He was at least a foot taller than me with shining hair and sharp features. His armor was absolutely pristine and was solid gold wrapped in irregular but intentional patterns around his arms and torso. There were no marks or scratches on any part of the armor, but something about the gray in his eyes made it clear that this angel had seen his fair share of war.

"Hi," I said, wondering if he was eyeing my bag of tasty snacks.

"Come with me," he said. That may seem abrupt, but

from the bit of personality I could discern in our three-second relationship, I guessed it was probably cordial by his standards.

Having learned better than to ignore such requests, I tossed the snacks into my car and followed the angel out to the sidewalk. He walked two paces in front of me, leading along the main street that ran in front of my apartment. He stopped to look both ways at each crossing, which made me laugh.

The last bit of sun was giving way to the yellowish glow of street lamps and headlights, reminding me that walking alone down this particular street at night was not especially wise. This drew my attention to the double-sided spear that hung across the angel's back. Each end was crowned by a flat, leafy blade that looked both decorative and immensely sharp. Looking at it put me at ease.

We made our way down two and one-half blocks. A steady flow of traffic kept things noisy on our right, while varying degrees of low-income housing formed the derelict scenery to our left. Without word or signal, the angel suddenly stopped. His reasoning quickly became clear.

While every house along the sidewalk was lit by outdoor lights, or at least the gentle flicker of a television near a window, the house that the angel had decided to stop at was in complete darkness. A wrought iron fence closed off the dilapidated yard, and a sickly black cloud covered the roof. A twisted arch made of the same darkness that covered the roof hung over the gate, adding to the palpable sense of malice that emanated from every inch of the place.

"Well," I said, turning to my angelic companion, "what

do we do?" Secretly I began writing my list of excuses if the plan had anything to do with me going into the dark house.

Much to my relief, the angel responded by pulling the double-ended spear from his back. A single slash sent a bolt of light into the front door. Wind rushed past me and blew the darkness away, as easily as smoke. The streetlights seemed lighter with the darkness gone, the malign weight no longer pressing against my chest.

Perplexed, I turned to the angel and asked, "What did you need me for? I didn't do anything."

This made him smile for the first time since he'd arrived. "I wouldn't have been allowed to be here if you didn't come with me."

∾

The kingdom of God is a place of pervasive life and perpetual activity. Everything is moving, everything has a story, and everything is alive. Looking into the spirit realm is like looking into a thriving rainforest—life upon life upon life. Devoid of the infinite layers of moss-coated trees, massive ferns, the cacophonous chatter of frogs and insects, and the multidimensional canopy that encapsulates it all, the landscape of a rainforest would be something entirely different. When I talk about angels, people seem to be under the impression that there are only a few, or at least only a few in any one place at a time. The opposite is true. Angels are everywhere, and most of them are activation angels.

Activation angel is a very broad term. There are easily

hundreds of different kinds, and I see them more frequently than any other type of angel. This category covers angels that carry healing, restoration of relationships, financial blessing, governmental transformation, social change, business ideas, inventions, peace, breakthrough, and dozens upon dozens of other things that we cry out to God for. So you may be wondering why I would lump such a diverse set of angels into a single group. Though what they are bringing can be a wide variety of things, activation angels all bring pieces of heaven to earth. They are all always looking for people who are ready to receive what they are bringing, but sadly, they don't always find people ready or willing to take it.

It's not just with angels. I walk into churches and see mountains of financial help piled next to those in need. I see fatherly love for the brokenhearted and lonely—not the intangible idea of distant affection from an impersonal deity, but a love more present and real than if God were physically standing in front of you with arms open wide. I see books full of wisdom and clarity flying directly into the hands of those seeking answers from heaven. I see the release of supernatural physical healing welling up from the ground near those who are in physical pain.

Every time I've prayed for someone to be physically healed—every single time—I've seen the healing available. Sometimes it's an activation angel carrying a bowl full of green liquid or a churning wave of light and color that splashes and splatters every corner of the room, but it's always there in some form. Unfortunately, not everyone I've prayed for has been healed. I've seen a fair share of hurt backs, broken bones, tumors, and ulcers healed on the spot. Yet I still have a similar list of people who left without being healed.

Sometimes I know why it didn't happen. I'll see a spirit of unforgiveness leeching on their necks. I might be experiencing a tangible lack of faith, or maybe they'll be engaging a mind-set or sin issue that prevents them from receiving the healing God has for them. Other times I can see no reason why the healing isn't happening. Faith is up on both sides and attitudes are good. There's no sense of sin or unforgiveness getting in the way, and there's an angel standing over the individual with a bucket of healing oil and a look of anticipation on his face. And yet sometimes it just doesn't happen.

This is one of my great frustrations. When these situations occur, people often resign to the idea that God doesn't want to heal them. Or they think the timing isn't right, or that perhaps He has some greater purpose for their ailments. None of these excuses satisfy the wealth of divine healing I see filling storehouses in the church, the anointing that pours from heaven in response to our prayers, or the angels crying, "God wants you to be healed more than you are capable of wanting anything!"

I have seen similar situations with every other kind of breakthrough we ask God for, be it financial, relational, or otherwise. It shows up for us to receive, carried by an activation angel or in some other way. Sometimes people receive it, sometimes they don't for reasons that are clear, and sometimes they don't receive it and there is no clear reason why.

I see activation angels more often than any other kind. When I'm at a church that knows God wants to actively and continuously pour out His love on them, these angels are soaring through the crowd doling out endless gifts, blessings, and impartations. Tragically, in most settings, I see these angels waiting. Whether it's for someone to send them, someone to open up their heart and mind, or someone to take ownership of their city or neighborhood—the angels wait for someone who knows what God has given to His people.

DEEP HEAVEN ANGELS

I was in the middle of a Sunday night service at Bethel Church in Redding when I suddenly had to leave. It was as urgent as the need for a bathroom while on a road trip and as subtle as a whisper in a windstorm, but I knew I had to go. Whether you're in a movie theater, airplane seat, or the middle of a church auditorium, there's no polite way to scoot past a full row of people. I did my best to avoid making any more eye contact than was necessary as I knocked knees with every person blocking my way to the aisle. From there it was a straight shot out the back door.

I immediately regretted leaving my sweatshirt at home as the air bit into my bare arms with merciless, cold teeth. Thinking that my car would at least block out the wind, I made my way up the small hill toward the gravel parking lot—arms crossed against the cold and eyes on my feet. I was halfway up the hill when I realized I wouldn't be making it to my car.

His light shone on the ground in front of me, but I felt his warmth before I saw the light. Hesitant, I lifted my gaze to see a pair of burning feet, flaming legs, and a blazing torso. To say he was engulfed in flames would be an understatement. The fire raged around him so thickly and violently that I wasn't able to tell if there was an angel somewhere in there or if this was a being made entirely of roaring flame.

This was imposing enough, but it was not the fire that gave me pause. Instead it was the immense sense of power and prestige that emanated from something inside the flames.

"Hello," I said, unable to think of a more regal greeting.

Again, it is important to note that whenever I've heard an angel speak, it hasn't been with actual words. Ideas, whole and complete, land in my brain. I can more or less translate these into an English sentence, but in my mind it is an understanding.

"Hello," the angel replied. A more dramatic reply was unnecessary, given his appearance.

"Something I can help you with?" I asked.

At this, the angel pulled a scroll from somewhere behind his back. It was in an ornate case that changed color the way a scarf waves in the wind. He pulled it open, revealing a dark, almost black, blue page with hundreds and thousands of intersecting lines, dots, and circles. In my memory it seems chaotic, but in the moment it was clear that every line was exactly in the place it was meant to be.

"What is it?" I asked.

"It is God's plan as it relates to you."

Then I noticed that all the lines and dots were slowly moving, orbiting, and growing. Dots blinked in and out of existence as connections were made and lost between people. Lines twisted and crossed as every possible choice that every person on the scroll could make interacted with every possible response to every possible choice. My eyes stretched open to maximum. The more I stared, the more I understood. The infinite complexity unfolding before me began to press against the borders of my mind. It was too much for my finite brain to comprehend, but I was still trying.

Frightened that I might burst a vital synapse, I shook my eyes free from the scroll and turned back to the angel. It was much easier to see him now—not the flame but the figure beneath. He wore golden armor with molded murals that covered every exposed surface. They clearly told a story, though the plot and characters were unclear to me. Perhaps this was just because I was still picking up the pieces of my blown mind. Every inch of him glistened. I want to say that his armor was inlaid with jewels and gems, but this looked nothing like it would on a necklace or engagement ring. Those kinds of jewels are held in place by fixtures and fastenings, but these were a part of the gold, just as leaves are a part of the tree. Nothing held them together. They were a part of each other.

I spent a lot of time admiring his armor, partially because it was so fascinating, but mostly because I was terrified to look this truly otherworldly being in the eye. At this point in my life I had seen many kinds of angels. Some of these had been intimidating—even alarming—but this was the first time I understood why certain angels began their message to man with "Be ye not afraid."

Fear is not the exact word I would use to describe the sensation that caused my knees to shake as I looked at this burning angel, but it certainly wasn't far off. I felt, in that moment, much as I think I'd feel if I opened my front door on a Saturday afternoon to discover that the president of the United States had shown up for lunch, only to find me wearing an old T-shirt and overused pajama pants and surrounded by empty pizza boxes and a vague odor of socks.

This feeling only magnified when I looked into his eyes. This angel had seen God as I had never seen Him. I met God before I could pronounce words like omnipresent, all-powerful, eternal, and holy. I had only ever known Him as the loving Father, faithful friend, and patient teacher.

I saw all these things and more in the burning angel's eyes. I saw the God who chose to let Himself love the fickle-minded people who lived on the planet He built with a breath. I saw the God who conceived ideas like time, gravity, economy, and glory. I saw the God who caused Moses's face to shine so brightly that it had to be hidden.

Looking in his eyes made me feel challenged and ashamed, so I directed my next comment to his feet: "The plans on that scroll look complicated."

This made him laugh. He grabbed both sides of the scroll and turned it horizontally and on its side, as if it were on a table between us. The lines and markings on the page sunk down into several layers below the surface of the paper, causing every dot and connection to twist and pulse in three dimensions.

My still feeble brain struggled to grasp what this meant and how this affected the bits and pieces that I'd under-stood when the scroll was just in two dimensions. Like an old bicycle desperately trying to snap into gear, my mind did its best, but the chain fell off. It all just looked like a tangled mess of intersecting lines and dots. All I knew was that God's plan was deeper, denser, more pliable, and more perfect than I was capable of comprehending.

I spoke with the angel for what seemed like a long time, though in truth it could have just as easily been ten minutes as four hours. We talked about what kinds of things were coming up in my life and the lives of my closest friends. I met with him twice after that, each meeting instigated by a whispered invitation while I was doing something else.

I've met several more of what I've come to call "deep heaven" angels after that day. I don't know if there are deeper and shallower parts of heaven, and apart from the meeting-the-president-in-my-pajamas feeling that I get, I've observed no common identifier between them. However, like a coal shot from the hottest part of a fire into a cold room, these angels all resonate with the heat of one who has been near the source of all warmth.

STRUCTURES

THE SPIRIT REALM is a real place. It's not a fleeting idea or some ambiguous feeling in our hearts. It is not a manifestation of our Christian ideals, experiences, or beliefs. Instead it is the source of them.

The relationship between the realm of the spirit and the physical realm is not so different from the relationships between different realms in the physical. I may not spend a great deal of time in the "realm" of the ocean, but I would be foolish to think what happens there has no effect on me.

I can dump all of my toxic waste into the ocean so that it doesn't muck up my living room, but when that waste eventually comes back to visit me through the tap or a can of radioactive tuna, I will begin to realize how connected to the ocean I am. The spirit realm may seem like some distant, ethereal plane that only affects our side of things in the form of a warm, tingling sensation during worship. But the truth is it never leaves you, and you never leave it.

You may not be aware of it, but you exist in the spirit realm just as much as you exist in the physical. You are 100 percent there and 100 percent here. Since the circumstances in our physical lives are usually more apparent than those of our spiritual lives, we are often distracted from our spiritual existence. That does not mean we are there any less. In fact, we are constantly affecting the spiritual atmosphere around us with our thoughts, actions, and mind-sets.

Human beings, more so than any other creature on the planet, have an immense capacity for affecting their environment. This is also true of the spiritual environment. If I were to till the soil in my backyard, plant tomato seeds, and nourish the seedlings that sprout from them, I would have created an environment where tomatoes can thrive. The spirit realm is not so different.

If I regularly worship in my home, then I have created an environment where the presence of God is attracted and can thrive. If I consistently get into angry arguments with my wife, then I have created an environment where the spirit of division and strife can thrive. These actions and thought patterns determine our spiritual environment.

A good friend of mine let my new wife, April, and I use his house the week after we got back from our honeymoon. He and his wife were out of town that week anyway, and it would still be a while before our apartment would be ready. This friend of mine—we'll call him John—was working on growing his gift of seeing in the spirit. And he had left notes all throughout his house where he had sensed or seen spiritual things.

A note next to the staircase read, "Small pot-like thingy." Next to the bit of paper was a squat ceramic pot with painted geometric shapes around its circumference. Inside was a thick, green liquid swishing from side to side as though it was excited to get out.

I had seen a similar green liquid present when people

would pray for physical healing. This made a great deal of sense to me. John had just completed his first year at the Bethel School of Ministry, and the pursuit of supernatural physical healing was a big part of that experience.

From there I noticed another note stuck to the wall behind the couch: "A shimmery waterfall all along here." The water was coming down too smoothly for me to accurately call it a waterfall. It poured out of the seam between wall and ceiling in a perfect sheet. It caught the light in unusual ways, bending the rays into odd patterns on the wall. I got the impression that the patterns were some kind of writing, though the characters and structure were foreign to me.

Even though the water came down in a thin film, it gave the impression of great depth. It clearly had to do with the depth of revelation that John was pursuing. I later found out that he spent his mornings deep in the Bible with piles of study books scattered across his workspace.

I found the last note in his room: "A big swirling vortex above our bed." This is common in most Christian households. I suppose that since our spirits don't need to sleep, they continue to pursue God as we rest. I imagine this is much easier without our minds to get in the way. This nightly communion cuts a clean path between heaven and our hearts, like the path that would appear if you continually poured water down a sand dune. People have taken to calling these pathways an "Open Heaven." My only problem with this is that the name suggests that heaven is closed everywhere except for these select few locations, which is entirely untrue. However, it's obnoxious to call these areas a "Slightly More Open Heaven" or a "Nice and Tidy Little Pathway to Heaven," so I suppose "Open Heaven" will do.

When I was exploring my friend's house, I was seeing what he had built in his environment through his continual pursuit of the Lord. "Structure" is the title I've given to the spiritual environment that we cultivate around us, the environment our thoughts and actions create. Everything, from the pagan rituals held by a coven of witches to the bedtime prayers of a toddler, creates a mark on the land. If such thought patterns and actions are consistent, then they will begin to alter the environment—much like how regular droplets of mineral-rich water from the ceiling of a cave will build a stalagmite.

∽

When I was eleven, I had a friend I'll call Rob. He lived off a dirt road in a house that smelled damp. Rob had been diagnosed with attention deficit disorder—this was just when that sort of thing was coming into vogue. He had to take remedial math and English classes, and the other kids had no problem reminding him of it. We hung out together at recess most days, but I only visited his house once.

At this point in my life I was only just realizing that there were things I saw that others didn't, but I had already learned to keep my mouth shut about them. So when we walked into Rob's room and I saw a demon hanging over his bed, I didn't bother mentioning it. It didn't look all that different from a tree sloth, if tree sloths were made of black mold and filthy yellow teeth.

It hung from a hank of dark moss that grew all over the space above Rob's bed, making it difficult to distinguish where the moss ended and the sloth-like demon began.

Looking back, I wonder if the smell of damp was caused by the age of the house or if I had actually smelled it in the spirit. My understanding of the spirit realm at the age of eleven, minimal as it was, did not clue me in as to what the sloth was doing over Rob's bed. However, after hearing a few harsh comments from Rob's father about his schooling and an embarrassed retort from his mother, I began to get the picture.

A culture of shame had been bred in that house. This environment created a situation where a demonic entity, intent on worsening Rob's condition, had access to his most private quarters.

CHURCH

I**T'S TIME FOR** a church service. I've been up since six getting a case of heavy computer equipment and myself ready for church. After a drowsy drive and a poor parking job, I walk into the sanctuary. The room does little justice to the amazing people who fill it, but there is charm in that.

I assemble my portion of the audiovisual equipment as quickly as possible so that I can get to writing. Over breakfast I decided to catalog everything that happens during worship because it might be interesting.

Three angels are pacing up and down the rows of chairs, swirling their arms in wide arching patterns that send little blue pellets of water from their fingertips. Their long, green robes add to the whimsical quality of their movements and seem to be soaked with the same water they sprinkle throughout the sanctuary.

The worship team practice goes no different than usual. People are discussing which key would be most appropriate for this song and when the best time for the drums to come in on that song is, but for some reason I can feel a growing sense of anticipation. This isn't because of the angels. They, or others like them, prepare the sanctuary every Sunday.

As the service gets closer, people start piling in. A momentum builds during practice, and the presence of God starts to enter the room. Then the first real song starts and it feels like the song hits a brick wall. I used to find this part of worship frustrating. This initial resistance happens almost every time.

I used to blame this resistance on the members of the congregation—secretly of course, because that sort of thinking isn't very Christian. Now I tend to think that this resistance is a natural force in and of itself. Climbing a mountain is a strenuous and difficult process that requires much effort, patience, and skill. You won't hear a mountain climber complain about this, however. They will be too busy telling you how fantastic the view from the top is. I think that sometimes an initial struggle makes the result more valuable.

I see three new angels standing at the front of the room—each head and shoulders above anyone on the stage. They struggle to raise their muscular arms as if they are trying to lift something immensely heavy, though I don't see anything in their hands. As they strain against this invisible force, I see that small green plants have sprouted in the places where the swirling angels sprinkled those pellets of water. The plants grow and shrink in sync with the large angels' attempts to lift their arms. I get the impression that they are struggling against the very same resistance that I feel whenever worship starts. It is as if they are trying to pull life from the ground.

One of our worship leaders steps up to the microphone to start the first song. I like this guy. I can see his heart from where I'm sitting; it burns white-hot, glowing in a way that stings my eyes. Will knows about purity. He doesn't care how high or steep the mountain is; he just wants to get to where God is waiting. And he wants to bring everyone with him. Whatever touched that heart would instantly incinerate and go up in smoke, like incense to heaven. A heart like his can turn anything into worship. The presence of God has always come during every worship service I have ever attended, but I am constantly amazed at how significantly the posture of our hearts affects our ability to feel that presence.

I still feel the resistance by the time the first song ends, but the angels' plants have grown to the ceiling and have begun to twist around the fluorescent lights like ivy.

The second song begins, and the second worship leader takes the lead. The moment she opens her mouth, I feel as if I'm being yanked up into the air. The wall behind the worship team begins to take on the texture and color of clouds and sunshine. The plants that had grown earlier begin to release large pieces of pollen that swirl through the air in time with the music.

Near the end of the song, she starts singing a simple prophetic song, "Sons and Daughters." Strength and encouragement appear out of thin air and strap on to people in the congregation like pieces of glowing red armor. It sinks into their skin and melts into their bones.

During the third song there is such a strong sense of being drawn into the loving heart of God that I forgot to write for the first half of the song. It's a real face-to-face moment with God. I can't see anything when I look around the room. Most of the angels have gone, but when

I focus on one person at a time, I see Jesus standing with him or her.

We humans have a different relationship with God than the angels do. I don't always understand the difference, but sometimes, when His presence takes on a certain quality, all the angels leave. Then it's just God and us.

A woman in the third row is holding her hands over her heart. Jesus stands directly in front of her, taking her hands in His as He whispers in her ear. A man is lying in the aisle with his face planted firmly in the carpet. Jesus kneels over him and rests both hands on his back.

Jesus is visiting each person individually yet all at the same time. Most are interacting with Him in one way or another—dancing, crying, laughing, or simply standing hand in hand. Others are scanning the room with a bored look on their faces or sitting with arms crossed. Jesus is standing near them too, of course, just waiting. He doesn't look frustrated or even disappointed. He's just waiting.

I'm going to stop writing for a minute because Jesus is standing in front of me too.

Laura must be sensing that some are not engaging in the available encounter with Jesus. The pain my heart feels when I see people ignoring Him is coming through her voice as she asks everyone to embrace the moment. She prays for everyone to be drawn deeper into His presence, and the feel of the worship changes from individual, personal ministry to a sense of corporate awe.

A massive throne appears above the band, and instantly I feel the entire congregation pulled into worship, just like the needle of a compass is inevitably pulled north. I personally believe that worship is an innate facet of our genetic makeup; that is to say, we are wired to recognize God when He enters the room. And when He does, our hearts start singing love songs before our mouths even have time to open.

Honestly, there is nothing particularly impressive about the throne apart from its size, but the sense of power emanating from it makes me feel scared to look at it for long. Jesus leaves His post with each person and takes His place in the stone chair. Now I am not afraid to look at the throne; I'm incapable. It feels like the entire room is being gravitationally pulled toward the spot where Jesus sits. The plants that grew at the beginning of worship send more tufts of pollen drifting gently through the room.

During the fourth song, the sense of corporate worship continues but changes direction. Instead of feeling frozen in awe at the power of God, I feel compelled to declare His goodness back at Him. The pollen that has been floating around the room catches fire. Each piece burns a different color and lights up like the embers that float from a campfire. They all begin to swirl upward, and the angels suddenly return. I can't tell whether it's the angels or the people packed around the stage who start it, but the worship transitions to dancing. A celebratory air follows the transition into dance.

During the fifth song, Jesus returns, meeting with each person individually again. A few people are still not acknowledging His presence, but it is much fewer people than before. Worship quickly changes from intimate conversation to celebration. Jesus begins dancing around the room wildly, along with all the angels.

One of our associate pastors gets up and begins to

prophesy, letting everyone know about the opportunity that is available. A large, muscular angel stands behind her as she speaks, smashing the ground with a massive sledgehammer. With every stroke the hammer sends ripples through the atmosphere, launching clouds of dust as well as many of the multicolored embers that have settled on the ground.

The pastor invites the congregation to sing the last song one more time. Naturally this explodes into another massive dance party. The band starts singing another prophetic song, "Chains are breaking off. Chains are breaking off... Veils are coming down. Veils are coming down." It would have been slightly more accurate to sing, "Chains are exploding into lots of teeny-tiny pieces... Veils are catching fire and then being completely incinerated." But I suppose that wouldn't have fit very well with the tune.

As everyone dances, chains that had been wrapped around about a fifth of the people in the room begin heating up until they are white-hot—a curiously similar white-hot to the burning hearts of Will and Laura Stern. Then the chains explode into pieces that disintegrate before they touch the ground. A veil that hangs over people's faces is being burned into nonexistence. All this, combined with the colorful embers floating on the wind, dancing angels, and dancing people, paints a clear picture of what I expect an average day in heaven looks like.

Cannon blasts of light and color erupt from the drum set as the drummer hammers out a final drum solo. Jesus takes armfuls of the light and casts it into the crowd, laughing hilariously the whole time.

The pastor scheduled to speak this morning is laid out flat

somewhere near the front row. We push our way through the announcements and offering, interrupted only by the occasional groan from the corner where the pastor is lying. I stand on my chair to get a better look and see that Jesus is hunched over him, pressing both hands on his chest.

After he's introduced, the pastor clambers most of the way to his feet and begins to speak. A rushing liquid light is spinning around his body like a tornado. Every few seconds the light rushes down his mouth and shines through his chest, causing him to go into another fit of groaning. Understandably, most of what he says is not in complete sentences, and a good deal of it is served from the floor. Regardless, what he has to say is one of the most powerful messages I've ever heard him give.

∾

This is a picture of what goes on in the spirit world in my church. I find church fascinating. I've been attending one church or another for as long as I can remember, and not a single one has been like any other. I've actually considered writing an entire book just about the kinds of things that go on in the spirit realm in different kinds of churches.

People who have been going to church for as long as I have are usually so jaded by their experiences that they are looking for any excuse to get out, or they have become so accustomed to tepidity of attending the weekly ritual that any alteration in routine comes as an offensive shock.

This is a gross generality, but one that I find too often to be true. There are exceptions, however. I think that the same dissatisfaction that compels people to quit attending church has motivated a great number of individuals to pursue new and more vibrant ways of expressing their adoration for God.

Don't think that I'm digging at traditional church. I often find that the people who spend their time speaking out against the structure of the church are operating from the same religious spirit they are trying to condemn. They are, after all, assuming that one structure is inherently more pleasing to God than another. While I'm sure that there are examples where this is true, the whole purpose of a church is to create a place where God's people can connect, be equipped, celebrate each other's victories, and worship God together.

After more than ten years of actively pursuing a deeper understanding of the gift of seeing in the spirit, I have come to one conclusion: there is way too much. There is too much joy, too much glory, too much of God's presence, too many good things that He has to say to His children. There are too many miracles ready to happen, too many breakthroughs, too many victories; there is too much restoration. There is way too much good for any one person or any group of people.

I believe that what God is doing on the earth is too big for any one church or any one denomination of churches. The things that are happening in the spirit are too big, and too good, for only a few people to be able to see it. I didn't try to fit every good thing or even every kind of good thing I have seen into this book. That would probably be impossible. I picked a few key stories so that you could have a taste of what's out there. Because I believe that God wants you to see what is happening in the spirit too.

MY STORY

ACT THREE

DIDN'T REALIZE IT at the time, but at the age of eighteen, my life was slowly churning in a cycle of aimless depression. After experiencing what I considered to be overwhelming opposition every time I tried to share my gift, I resolved to keep what I saw just between God and myself.

I would occasionally share some visions with my closest friends and family, but only if they pressured me. This worked out well enough, for the most part. Discussing the things I saw with the Holy Spirit always led to enlightenment and peace, and any attempt to share my gift with people led to confusion and frustration. Removing the pressure of trying to use my gift for the benefit of others made life less complicated. Life, however, did not accommodate my complacency for long.

My youth pastor, whom I had grown close to in recent years, was sent to start a new ministry in Los Angeles. Though I felt more connected to him than any other leader in the church, I knew that I wasn't supposed to go with him. Many of my closest friends decided to go to the Bethel School of Supernatural Ministry in Redding, California, but I had no desire to do so.

I had been to Bethel, the church that had started the school, several times by then. I'd attended several of their conferences, and though it was clear that the Spirit of God dwelled there, I had no desire to enroll in the school. This, I suppose, was mostly due to the comfort I'd found in the stagnation that had come to my life. I knew that if I went to the school, I would be surrounded by the same kind of Spirit-starved people who caused my current internal reclusion. So I had my answer ready when the Holy Spirit tapped me on the shoulder and told me that I should go to the school: "No thanks."

He asked at least a dozen times that summer. I made sure to mix up my responses so He didn't get bored:

- "That's all right. I think I'll go to college instead."

- "Maybe I'll consider it next year."

- "Why would I go to a ministry school when I can just talk to You?"

- "I didn't want to go into ministry in the first place."

- "I think I'll become an English teacher."

None of my arguments convinced Him. He remained consistently polite and undemanding without losing any resolve: "You should go to that school."

After months of this the deadline to send in my application came and went. I didn't go.

Actually, I didn't do much that year. I started college, finished my first novel, and watched every episode of *The Simpsons,* but none of it came with much satisfaction. God remained warm and encouraging, sending pictures of success and achievement that flitted through my mind's eye.

Despite the sense of kindness that came with these images, I couldn't help but be irked by them. I guess that this constant encouragement served as a continual reminder that I was completely ignoring a significant portion of my identity. So I started shutting out the Holy Spirit.

Having spent the previous six years building a constant line of communication between Him and me, this proved difficult. In the end I found myself regularly in my room, simultaneously playing one video game or another, watching a movie on my computer, and blasting music through my headphones.

The year I won the argument with God, one of my best friends moved up to Redding to attend the school of ministry. She would call me from time to time, playfully berating me for not going to the school and sharing in all the fabulous testimonies of healing and supernatural power that she and all my friends were experiencing there. She knew, of course, how strongly averse I was to going.

One night, while I was once again surrounded by a cacophony of blaring guitar riffs, witty dialogue, and rapidly exploding pixels, the Holy Spirit spoke to me again. His voice came so quietly that it would have been simple to miss, but it resonated with my spirit so profoundly that it was impossible to ignore. "You know, you should really go to this school." I had probably heard Him say that fifty times, but for whatever reason this time instantly melted every wall, barricade, and rampart I had built against the idea.

Three seconds later, while I was still busy staring at the puddle that had been my hardened heart, Michelle called. She started the conversation with, "You know, you should really come to this school."

My elaborate defenses lying in splinters at my feet, I said, "So why don't you tell me about it?"

∾

Though my resistance to the school failed, the resolve to keep my gift under wraps grew even more resilient. "All right, God," I said the day I sent in my application, "I'll go to this school of Yours, but I am not telling a single person about what I see." Since He put up no argument, I assumed that my terms were acceptable.

I managed to keep my secret for the majority of my first year, though God was certainly working on opening me up. The group of fellow Bethel students that I roomed with were the perfect combination of prying and safe. Each contributed in his own perfect way, conversationally pick-axing their way through all my walls. By the end of the school year my defenses were in shambles. I only needed a final swing of the hammer to bring them crashing down. That hammer came in the form of a simple prophetic word from a friend.

It was missions time, when all the Bethel students got the opportunity to traverse the globe to heal the sick, raise the dead, and generally do what Bethel students do. Since I had no money, I went on the least expensive trip, one traveling to Tijuana, Mexico. Most students don't have money, so the Tijuana trip was one of the most popular. This resulted in a large caravan cruising down Interstate 5 from Redding to Mexico. Since said caravan was made up of Bethel students, we spent the majority of the drive relaying prophetic words between cars over handheld radios. Near the end of our journey, a familiar voice came through the static.

"Blake, this one's for you," said my friend. "God says that it's time to come out of the cave." Then the radio clicked off. It was a simple word, but it hit like a cannonball to the chest. It simultaneously knocked down the remnants of my old defenses and gave me the courage to share the things that I saw. Most uncharacteristically, I started right away.

Upon arriving at our destination, a small Christian camp just outside the city of Tijuana, I told a few fellow students what I saw during the worship service we held that evening. I talked with some of the leaders about the angels who were drifting around the camp, and I even told a few people what their personal angels looked like. This was the most I'd shared in several years, but the real kicker came halfway through the trip.

Since nearly three hundred students had come down from Bethel, it would have been cramped to the point of insanity to mash us all into one of the local churches, which typically held somewhere between twenty and fifty members. Instead, we broke up into small teams and went to several churches around the area.

During the day, my team went out to the area surrounding the church, inviting people to the service we would be holding that night and praying and healing as we went. As my team and I did this, I decided to look in the spirit so that I could share what I saw with the church.

The service had already been going well by the time I approached the stage. Several had been healed of everything from back pain to chronic ulcers, and the crowd

131

was excited for more. Someone handed me the microphone, and in the stop-and-go way you speak through a translator, I shared what I'd seen.

The town was situated in a sloping valley. As I walked through the mishmash of particleboard buildings that lined the trash-strewn streets, I saw the blood of Jesus flowing down the valley. This may sound like a scene from a horror movie, but the blood was simultaneously shimmering gold and crystal clear, like water in the Caribbean. I saw two large angels near the church entrance—each at least twenty feet tall, wearing ornate robes and carrying intricately detailed weapons. When I looked at the ceiling of the sanctuary, I saw (in the spirit) that the building had no roof. Nothing was separating them from what God was pouring on them.

As I described this, the translator began to weep, and the entire congregation joined him. This surprised me. Sure, the things that I saw were pretty cool, but this sort of thing was around every church. It varied from place to place, of course, but there was always something neat.

The translator, who also turned out to be the pastor, composed himself. "You don't understand. This man was sent by God," he said, pointing a shaking hand in my direction.

Naturally this made me feel quite awkward. I supposed that it was technically true, but everyone is "sent by God," if you think about it.

"Everything you said," he continued, staring directly into my eyes, which did not help put me at ease. "Everything, word for word, is exactly what we've been praying."

Then he addressed the crowd, though he kept speaking

in English: "We prayed that the blood of Jesus would flow through this valley. We asked God to send powerful angels to guard our doors. We prayed that our church would be fully open to heaven."

I stood frozen on the stage, blown away by a simple truth that had somehow eluded me all these years. These people didn't know that God was with them. Yes, they *believed* that God was with them. They had seen miracles and healing, received prophetic words, and felt His presence flow in their midst, but they didn't know just how *with them* God was.

Maybe I knew it because I'd grown up surrounded by ministry, maybe my family's positive and encouraging nature influenced me, or maybe my unique gift had made it impossible for me to miss the fact that God's hand is in everything. Whatever the reason, I never realized that people who knew God might not know how close His kingdom is.

It had been sitting right in front of my face my whole life, but I had been either too dull or too self-absorbed to see it. When people asked me question after question after question, when they followed me to my car and offered to take me out to dinner, when they begged me to impart the gift of seeing—all they wanted was to see what God was doing. I had somehow made it through life with the assumption that they all knew.

Through all the bumps and bruises that I had received while trying to learn how to use my gift, the only time anything ever worked or made sense was when I sat with God and spoke with Him about what I saw. It worked so well while everything else about my seeing perpetually failed that I came to value this connection with God above all else. It had become so intrinsic to everything I did that I couldn't imagine functioning without it.

People gave me prophetic words that made me feel really great, but they were a small footnote in the volumes-long love letter that God had been writing to me. Since what God had to say to me was the meat that fed my identity, I viewed what everyone else had to say as side dishes and desserts. I felt the same way about the things that I saw. They were neat and fun to look at, but I cared much less about them than what God had to say about them.

I assumed that anyone who could hear the voice of God would understand His kingdom. They wouldn't need to see it because hearing it from His mouth was the best part. This made me feel that everyone who dogged me to say what I saw or wanted me to give them an impartation was just greedy or obsessed with the novelty of seeing. As I stood completely stunned on that stage in Mexico, I realized that most people don't *know* God's kingdom—they know *about* God's kingdom.

I returned to Redding a few days later, still in a daze. I finally had something that was missing my entire life—a reason for seeing in the spirit. It was only a spark, but I knew that, given time, I would be able to grow that spark into a raging inferno.

When I arrived home, I had a challenge to face. Though many students had heard about what I had seen during the trip, I could easily play it off as a one-time fluke and return to my spiritual reclusion. But that spark had already begun to start a small fire in my heart. I decided the best way to keep the flames fanned would be to keep telling people that I saw in the spirit. Without thinking about it too much, I asked one of my friends if I could speak at her home group the following week.

∽

And that brings me to where I started earlier, full of panic staring at forty people crammed into a tiny apartment, all waiting for me to share my story. A student I'd never met was playing guitar, leading the group in a few worship songs, but I was too nervous to worship. I wrung my hands, trying to figure out what to say. I hadn't come up with anything by the time the last song ended, so I decided to say everything.

Over the course of about thirty minutes, I told the story of my life. It sounded strange, even to my ears. I had never told the whole story all at once like that. After I finished, the questions began.

This was the part I was dreading most. These questions were one of the main reasons I drove myself into seclusion.

"What is my angel doing now?"

"Do non-Christians have angels?"

"Can you see any demons on me?"

"Can you teach me to see angels?"

"Where is my angel when I'm in the bathroom?"

But for some reason those questions that used to confuse and annoy me suddenly brought inspiration. I had the answer to every single one. Unique illustrations and explanations of visions and revelations that I would have been at a loss to explain in the past came flooding to present memory.

Some part of me had assumed, though I knew that most people couldn't see in the spirit, that they must have some sense of their spiritual surroundings. Everything people had asked me in the past used to feel greedy and needy. Now it was easy to see their hearts. For the first time I didn't see this flood of questions as the overspiritualized fanaticism of hype-drunk zealots but the genuine hunger of those who had tasted God in part and been left wanting more.

That night I answered questions for three and a half hours. It was the first time I ever felt good about sharing the things I saw. Over the course of a single week I had gone from having no idea what to do with my gift to having an ever-growing list of ideas and opportunities about how to share it. In a single night I went from wondering why I could see in the spirit to wanting to teach others to see.

PART III

DO IT YOURSELF

HAVE BEEN OFFERED money, gifts, favors, jobs, dinners, and ministerial positions. I've been asked, begged, stalked, and threatened—all by people looking to receive the gift of seeing in the spirit. Since the day I first spoke about my gift, it's been abundantly clear that people are desperate for a taste of it. Unfortunately, I've been seeing in the spirit for as long as I can remember, so for quite a while I felt thoroughly unqualified to teach people how to do it. Seeing had always been as natural as breathing.

From the age of twelve to eighteen, I would go back and forth as far as sharing my gift. Even though I wasn't always comfortable sharing what I saw, I had an inborn conviction that my gift was meant to be available to anyone who knew God. So I would always pray for an impartation for anyone who wanted to see. By the time I was nineteen I'd prayed for about three hundred people to receive the gift of seeing in the spirit. Only two received it on the spot. I'm no statistician, but I'm fairly certain that those aren't good odds. Apart from a few angst-ridden teenage years, I never had a problem praying for anyone who asked, but I rarely saw more than the most meager fruit. People reported seeing streaks of light or the odd shadow out of the corner of their eye, but rarely more. I entered my second year at the school of ministry with the desire to change this.

My roommates and I hosted a home group every Wednesday night. I was preparing to share my story with all of them—the second time I had done so in front of a crowd—when an idea struck me. Whenever I imparted the gift of seeing in the spirit, I would say a simple prayer, lay my hands on the receiver, and hope for a good report later. In the school of ministry, when praying for someone to be healed, we were taught to ask them to test it out right away:

- "Jump on that leg."
- "Does it hurt when you twist your back like this?"
- "Could you try to take a few steps?"

All of those questions were designed to put the healing to an immediate test. This had been a crucial step toward seeing people healed of physical ailments, and it suddenly occurred to me that this could be part of the reason I hadn't seen much success with impartation.

Although the concept was sound, I didn't see how this would turn into anything but a group of people sitting in a circle taking turns and saying, "I don't see anything." Then I got another idea.

"All right, everyone," I said, having just finished my life story. "Here's what I want you to do. Stand up, and I'll lay my hands on each one of you to release the gift of seeing in the spirit."

I made my way through the twenty or so people in a few minutes. People sometimes get frustrated that I pray for such a short time when I impart. I tell them that I just pray until I see the gift land on them. I suppose I could pray longer and throw in a few scriptures from Isaiah or something, but that would just be for flair.

The truth is that the majority of the impartation happens while I'm talking about the things I've seen. As I share stories and experiences, I watch the anointing to see in the spirit leak out from me—just as I am sure the majority of the impartation from this book happened while you read through it. I just pray to seal what has already been done.

"So here is what I want you to do," I said, finishing my lap around the room. "I want you to close your eyes and ask the Holy Spirit where something in the room is. It can be an angel, open heaven, or whatever. Once you feel like you know where something is, look at that spot and ask the Holy Spirit to show it to you.

"If you see something with your eyes, that's great," I continued. "But if you don't see it that way, then try to look for it the way you would try to get a prophetic word or picture. Ask the Holy Spirit to show you in your mind's eye. It can even be a vague impression or a general idea of what it is. Use whatever gift you're comfortable with to perceive what's going on in the room. I'll give you two minutes."

Honestly, I didn't think it was going to work. Wanting to be ready in the unlikely scenario that it did, I took a quick inventory of the activity in the room. A protection angel stood vigil next to the front entryway, while a similar angel covered the sliding glass door to the backyard. A swirling vortex had opened a tunnel in the ceiling—a regular occurrence anytime I shared about seeing in the spirit. An ornate golden arch vaulted over the front door, pouring liquid light on anyone who passed the threshold.

All this was encased by a dense fog that, rather than obscuring the surroundings, made everything more visible. These were just the highlights, of course. Each person had his or her own unique angel with them, his or her personal spiritual ecosystem, and any number of other various lights and swirls floating around everyone.

The members of the home group looked around the room with squint-eyed intent. No one jumped out of his or her chair or began screaming wildly, so I figured that this new method hadn't been effective. Two minutes passed, and we started going around the circle. Everyone saw the typical things they always saw when I prayed for them: a brief flash of something on the wall, a streak of light over there, or a vague shadow out of the corner of his or her eye. What shocked me were the things that they saw *without* their eyes.

Three different people saw, in their minds' eyes, a picture of the protection angel by the front door. Two saw a shimmer over the entryway and had an impression of pouring water and imparted blessing. All told, 80 percent of the people in my living room had seen something that matched what I saw or what someone else in the room saw.

Since somewhere around 99 percent of my previous attempts had ended in disappointment, I was as shocked as anyone. Sure, everyone was only seeing the first scratches on the surface of the spirit realm with their eyes, but using the gifts that they were already comfortable with, God was revealing what was behind that flash of light or that ripple in the air.

I don't know why I hadn't thought of it before. The spirit realm is a real place, just as real as the physical realm. Chances are, the main way you experience the physical world is through your eyes, but that doesn't mean you don't receive a ton of information about the world around you with your other senses. In fact, I'd be willing to bet that if you were blindfolded and put to the task of describing the layout and contents of an unfamiliar room, you would emerge with at least a rudimentary idea of what was in it.

Since our spiritual senses are capable of being much more finely tuned than our physical ones, it stood to reason that anyone should be able to get a decent idea of their spiritual surroundings.

Please don't think that I'm trying to condemn you to the shallow end of the spirit pool. The more time I've spent instructing people in seeing, the more I've come to realize that learning to steward what you have is the quickest way to attain what you lack. By asking people to pursue an understanding of the spirit realm through the gifts they were already comfortable with, I was giving them something attainable.

Spiritual gifts are an expression of relationship with God. He gives them freely and does not remove them. They are not earned, but the quality of their growth and expression is in direct proportion to your divine relationship. By giving people a simple and practical way to pursue seeing in the spirit, I discovered a way to make seeing a part of their routine with God.

∽

The first key to seeing in the spirit is to look. This may seem painfully obvious, but it is one of the biggest reasons that people don't see. Whether it's because they don't think they'll see anything, are frightened of what they might see, or simply haven't thought about it—most people never make the attempt.

Regularly taking a moment to perceive what's happening in the spirit realm is one of the quickest ways to grow in it. I believe that it is ideal if you can work out the terms and methods of your pursuit of seeing on your own with the Holy Spirit. That is, let the Holy Spirit teach you how to see.

I realize that this is a vague bit of instruction, but the ability to commune with the Holy Spirit is paramount to your success in seeing, not to mention every other aspect of life. However, for those of you who find the ambiguity of "just let the Holy Spirit show you how to see" frustrating, here are the simple step-by-step instructions I gave to my home group:

1. Close your eyes and ask the Holy Spirit where to look.

You may hear a specific direction. You might suddenly picture a place in your mind. You may just get a vague impression toward a certain area. Typically when the Holy Spirit wants to show me something, I'll feel a gentle tugging sensation, like my equilibrium is subtly tipping in a certain direction. This part will vary from person to person. If for whatever reason you can't get a clear sense of where to look, just pick a likely spot. It's better to try and fail than to get all tangled in the details.

2. Open your eyes, look at the spot, and ask the Holy Spirit to show you what's there.

You may instantly see an angel with your physical eye. I would be lying if I said it happens all the time, but I've seen some pretty hilarious facial expressions on those occasions. Many people see a ripple in the air, like the heat distortion that comes off asphalt on a hot summer day. Some see a brief flash or a streak of light. Typically I'll see a glowing mass or indistinct shape, detail coming as I focus on it, though sometimes it's all immediately clear the moment I look. If you don't see anything, then look for it the same way you would an answer from the Holy Spirit or a prophetic word. A picture may come to your mind, or a sentence. Even an impression of joy or peace can be an indication of what occupies that space.

3. Ask the Holy Spirit to explain what you are seeing.

You're probably not going to get nature-documentary-style commentary explaining the peculiar behaviors and unique physiology of each angelic being you see, but I've found that the Holy Spirit is always excited to share about the inner workings of His kingdom. This, I feel, is the most important step in the process. It prevents seeing from becoming a mere novelty and helps make seeing in the spirit a method of deepening your relationship with God.

I recommend using this exercise, or whatever method you've invented for yourself, as often as possible. When you're sitting on the bus, waiting at an airport, stuck in heavy traffic, or sitting in the middle of worship, the spirit world is always alive and active. Every person I know who has pursued this gift consistently and made regular attempts at looking has steadily grown in seeing in the spirit.

POTENTIAL BLOCKAGES

NOW THAT I'VE been teaching people to see in the spirit for several years, I've found that most take to it naturally. As with anything having to do with God, certain forces are interested in keeping you from seeing. The demonic resistance is too meager to be bothered with for the most part, especially when viewed from our place in the arms of the King of all kings. Internal resistances are much more effective in preventing God's supernatural power and love from reaching our hearts or from recognizing it when it does.

I have listed a few of the key issues that will sabotage your ability to see in the spirit realm. Fortunately, every single one of these problems is best solved by the very thing that will hone your seeing gift: time spent communing with your Creator.

FEAR

The first tactic of the enemy is fear. Fear is faith in the devil—believing that God is incapable of protecting and guiding you. The devil has some power, but he has no authority unless you give it to him with your faith.

I am convinced that the torment I experienced as a

child was an aggressive attempt to frighten me away from the gift God gave me. I regularly meet people who had a similar experience to mine. Often they are afraid to pursue seeing again in case those frightening images return.

People who have never seen sometimes shy away from pursuing the gift after hearing some of the less pleasant things that I see, afraid that they won't be able to handle such dark visions. While it is true that some of what I see is grotesque and unpleasant, and the demonic entities that scared you away from your gifting may attempt to torment you again, none of this matters if you are closely connected to God.

Jesus died so that we could be close to God again. Everything was solved by that sacrifice. The most malevolent machinations of the enemy shatter against God's shins like a car made of matchsticks trying to ram a tank. The enemy is terrified of people who can see in the spirit because it reveals his powerlessness and God's greatness.

UNFORGIVENESS

If there is one thing that can prevent you from experiencing the goodness of God, it is unforgiveness. When we choose not to forgive, we are not allowing others the very thing that gave us access to God's presence. Jesus died on the cross as the answer to the laws of sin and death. It was the ultimate act of forgiveness. God looked at the entirety of human history, saw every dark choice that every person would make, and decided that we were worth forgiving.

That act of forgiveness is the only thing that allows His presence to enter our hearts. When you don't forgive, you have refused to view life from God's perspective. You may be able to see into the spirit realm with unforgiveness in your heart, but I guarantee that you will not be seeing it through God's eyes.

What is the solution? If you can't find the forgiveness you need for those who have wronged you, then look for it in the heart of the Father. You will find it there.

OFFENSE

Jesus had no problem offending people. He regularly called out the Pharisees for their religious beliefs in creatively confrontational ways. He told a Canaanite woman that she was a dog (Matt. 15:21–28). And He alienated the majority of His followers when He told them to drink of His blood and eat of His flesh (John 6:51–54). In all but one of these cases, people missed the blessing that Jesus had for them because they were offended.

The Pharisees were so stuck on protecting the religious prestige they had built for themselves that they were unable to see the Savior they had spent their lives studying. The crowd around Jesus left when He told them to drink and eat of Him because they couldn't hear the heart behind His words (John 6:53). The Samaritan woman, however, pushed past the potential offense and received the miracle she was looking for (Matt. 15:27–28).

Most offense comes from insecurity. Anything that challenges the identity that we create for ourselves or our current view of the world feels threatening.

The solution is twofold: become an expert at connecting with the Holy Spirit about everything that you don't understand, and make your relationship with God the core of your identity.

If you want to see in the spirit, you will see things that challenge your beliefs, perceptions, and identity. Alone, this is terrifying. When you're sitting in God's lap with His voice in your ear, it's exhilarating.

RELIGION

Through ritual and labor, religion is trying to achieve what God wants to give you through your relationship with Him. Real relationships are scary because in a true relationship, both parties are free.

My wife could decide she likes someone else more than me. I'm kidding myself if I think that quoting Scripture to her or preaching about the value of commitment is going to prevent her from making those kinds of decisions. Even the vows we spoke on our wedding day are not powerful enough to keep her from leaving me.

What keeps my wife from hurting me is the value that she has for my heart. She doesn't need someone to tell her that committing adultery is wrong. She knows that it would crush my heart. Through love and trust, we have built a security in our marriage that no rules or regulations could ever match. I gave her my heart, and she gave me hers. Now we get to protect them.

In the old covenant it was against the law to commit adultery. Jesus said that it is wrong to think about anyone lustfully (Matt. 5:27–28). In the old covenant it was against the law to kill someone. Jesus said that it is wrong to hate anyone (vv. 43–44). Did Jesus make the law stricter? No. He revealed the heart of it.

Jesus said that we are no longer slaves but friends (John 15:15). Paul wrote that we have been made coheirs with Christ because of the sacrifice Jesus made (Rom. 8:16–17). The punishments and rules have taken a backseat because God got what He was originally looking for—a place to give His heart.

The Bible is not a set of rules and regulations that must be followed to earn a place near God. It is a picture, painted over thousands of years, of God's pursuit of mankind. It is the story of the Bridegroom seeking His bride. Is He going to strike you with lightning or pull all His blessings from your life if you sin? Probably not. But He gave you His heart to protect.

Religion prevents you from seeing in the spirit because it puts a wall of regulation and duty where God intended to put love. It makes you a slave when He's looking for sons and daughters.

INDEPENDENCE

To be clear, I am not referring to your ability to function as a singular being in this section. I am also not talking about the declaration Americans celebrate on July 4. By "independence" I mean the spirit of division that makes you believe you don't need others.

This is one of the main attacks against all prophetic people. It is my belief that the prophetic is best expressed when under the covering of accountability and authority. You need people in your life to love and encourage you as well as warn you if you're swerving off the rails. Any gift or revelation that does not function within the context of loving godly relationships with other people is a gift or revelation that you should question.

Most of the prophets in the Bible followed this model,

serving in the priesthood or under a king. It was only in rare and extreme circumstances that they operated independently. Besides, people are going to value your revelations and experiences much more if they know who you are. It is difficult to know how to value a wild seer running around in the wilderness. However, if you are part of a community that has seen God's grace on your life, then your revelations have a context.

The main justification for spiritual independence is the idea that you can get all you need from God. While it is true that God is *capable* of filling every need you will ever have, I do not believe that this is His *intent*.

This was a big struggle for me while I learned how to use my gift. My interactions with other people regarding the spirit were constantly frustrating, while my conversations with God were fun and enlightening. The truth was, however, that by keeping my experiences to myself I was limiting the perspective I could have on the things I saw. While every answer is in the heart of God, I believe that He hides some of those answers in the people around us because He wants us to need each other.

Everything that God does is modeled on family. It is in this structure that growth and health flourish. You need spiritual fathers and mothers to speak into your life, brothers and sisters to run beside you, and children that you are pouring into. In this structure it is difficult to get far off track, and it's easy to grow.

EPILOGUE
WHY?

WHEN I WAS younger and more irritable, I asked people why they wanted to see in the spirit when they came to me looking for an impartation. This was partially because I was annoyed by the constant attention my gift brought and partially because it was a question I had been asking myself.

I got a lot of answers to my question:

- "Because I've always wanted to see."

- "Because I've always just felt things, and I think I'd feel less crazy if I could just see them."

- "Because I think it'd be fun to see angels."

None of these answers were bad, but none of them answered the question burning in my heart. Sure, it blessed people when I told them what their angels looked like, and it helped leaders when I shared what was happening during a meeting. But it wasn't enough.

These practical applications made me an effective servant but no more effective than the average talented prophetic person. I knew that there was some larger purpose to what I saw. As I should have guessed, it was written in every vision I'd seen since birth. It just took me twenty years of looking to see it.

THE VEIL

I went to a Soul Survivor conference in England when I was fifteen. It was the last part of a two-week European mission trip with my youth group. The three-day event was being held at a large cattle auction house. Most of the three thousand attendees were camping in tents on the cattle field that surrounded the structure.

On the last night of the conference I sat near the front of the upper deck that overlooked the mass of people. The main floor, which I assume would typically hold pens full of livestock, was packed with row after row of young people listening to Mike Pilavachi preach.

Years of church experience made it clear that he was winding up for an altar call. Having been saved for the majority of my life, I felt justified in my decision to ignore the remainder of the message and try to catch a few moments of precious sleep. It was then that I saw Jesus.

He was pacing back and forth in the space between where the stage began and the rows of chairs ended. He didn't look like the stereotypical bearded and robed Jesus that I had seen in so many Sunday school coloring books. Apart from the faint glow that engulfed His head, He would not have been out of place in line at the supermarket or in the classical literature section of a bookstore. But I knew it was Jesus the moment I saw Him, and it made me stand up.

He continued to pace, His gaze never diverting from a spot somewhere at the back of the room. Though it would have been impossible to do so under normal circumstances, I followed His line of sight the hundred or so yards to the back, where a young woman sat with her head slumped against the divider between the first row of stadium seats and the main floor.

"He sees no one but her," said a voice somewhere in my head.

The room began to fade as I watched Jesus pace. It wasn't that I couldn't see the room or hear Mike preaching, but I abandoned those things so that more and more of my focus could be placed on Jesus and the girl in the back. Even my awareness of my own body began to lessen. Distantly I heard Mike start the invitation for people to come to the front.

I felt more than saw the girl make the slightest movement as she tilted her head in response to him. I saw Mike move, but it took him no time to get from where he was pacing at the front of the stage to the divider at the back of the room. Jesus stood in front of her.

The room was all but gone, the kind words of the passionate preacher distant and muffled. I couldn't feel the ground beneath my feet because every inch of my consciousness was drawn to the scene below.

The girl lifted her head just enough to look Jesus in the eye. Immediately chains appeared around her neck, then her shoulders, and then her waist until she was covered, neck to knees. The chains extended from her in four long strings, a furious demon yanking at the end of each. The weight of them caused her to slump, but it didn't matter.

Jesus leaned forward and kissed her on the forehead. Every link in the chain split in half, starting at her neck and running all down her body like a string of firecrackers. The demons flew back from the loss of tension as the world flashed away in blinding white light.

My vision slowly returned, but the room did not. Instead there was only Jesus and the girl. The preacher and auction house were gone, and I felt no more substantial than a pair of disembodied eyes.

A lifetime of satisfaction was written on Jesus's face, and the girl now stood in long robes. It may be something of a Christian cliché, but the robes were whiter than white—the whitest thing I have ever seen, before or since. Jesus opened His arms and the girl lunged forward, sinking her face into His chest and wrapping her arms around His torso. I felt embarrassed, as if I'd stumbled into a wedding wearing baggy sweats and a stained T-shirt. Then I felt a weight form above me.

I looked up and saw a giant hand coming down from the sky. Each finger was thick as a baseball bat. The index finger extended and touched me on the forehead. As if I'd been dropped into a pool of ice water, I snapped back into reality with such force that I fell backward into my chair. I sat there a moment, feeling shorted out, and then I stood just in time to see the girl from the back running up the aisle to accept Jesus (even though she already had).

The rest of the meeting swept by in a misty blur. I didn't know it was over until people began pushing past me on their way to the exit. I got up to leave without really thinking about what I was doing. I fixed my eyes on one of the girls from my youth group to keep from getting lost in the flowing crowd.

I had spoken to her a half dozen times at our church in California but hadn't really gotten to know her any better on the trip. In a flash I saw the entirety of her life.

I saw every moment, felt every emotion, and could

not look away. I saw every choice she had made—good or bad—and the process that led to each decision. I saw every sin, every lie, and every mistake. I saw secret hopes, hidden dreams, and private prayers. I saw every moment of her future and then every possible future based on every decision she would or wouldn't make. I saw the full measure of her potential and how far she would make it within that potential. Emotions flooded faster than I could comprehend them. Triumph, loneliness, laughter, shame, hope, fear, warmth, sorrow, and elation all swirled and congealed into one impossibly profound whole—love.

This love was more complete than I had ever felt, the sum of every moment of a life viewed with adoring eyes. It was bigger than anything I'd ever perceived and simpler than anything I'd ever experienced. I suddenly understood why Jesus chose to die on the cross, and in that moment, I would have done the same.

Overwhelmed, I tore my vision from the girl, but my gaze snapped onto one of the guys in our youth group like a magnet. Again, an entire lifetime poured in through my eyes. Again, a love I couldn't explain or contain filled my chest until I yanked myself free to keep from bursting. Then my eyes caught one of the other random conference attendees. I'd never met him, but I knew everything that could be known about him.

I bounced from person to person, fighting to keep my brain from erupting. I wanted to prophesy, to sing, to preach, to grab each person by the cheeks and scream in their face, "You are loved!" But instead I just stumbled through the crowd, brokenhearted at how woefully inadequate any attempt at sharing this love would be.

I planted my chin on my chest and marched behind my youth pastor, staring at the ground. Then someone's foot crossed my field of view, and I saw everything about his life before I even saw his face. Somehow I made it back to my tent and fell face-first into my pillow.

∾

I've heard people say that there's no such thing as the "gift of seeing in the spirit." They say that people who see just have a very high level of "discerning of spirits." This used to bother me and still does to some degree. Mostly because I feel that we often spend too much time categorizing and defining gifts that were designed to be an expression of relationship with God. I don't mind the sentiment that seers are simply operating from a high level of discernment as long as we understand what the gift of discerning of spirits is.

It is commonly accepted that discerning of spirits is the act of identifying what is of God and what is of the devil. This is the most basic level of discernment. Any Christian who has even a remedial relationship with the Holy Spirit can identify the difference between something godly and something demonic. I believe it is the calling of every Christian to discern the *ways* of God.

A lot happened the moment Jesus died on the cross. The laws of sin and death were satisfied. The estranged relationship between God and man was restored to its original glory. And a veil was torn.

When teaching on this story, any preacher worth his salt will point out that the veil was ripped from top to bottom—at least five times. While there can be no doubt as to whose efforts caused the barrier between the holiest of holies and the rest of the temple to come down, there are varying thoughts on the implications of this powerful prophetic symbol. I can't help but think that God was saying that the barrier between His kingdom and ours—the kingdom of heaven and earth—had been removed. This, I suppose, is why Jesus spent so much time teaching His followers how to recognize the kingdom.

Jesus said to His disciples, "No longer do I call you slaves, for the slave does not know what his master is doing; but I have called you friends, for all things that I have heard from My Father I have made known to you" (John 15:15, NASB).

For the first nineteen years of my life, seeing in the spirit was a tremendously frustrating gift. The charm of seeing angels flit around was all but lost on me because I had never seen the world any other way. It's not that I didn't find it interesting in and of itself, but there never seemed to be any point apart from the novelty.

This thought process led me to resent those who so desperately wanted my gift, since I couldn't help but think that the only reason they wanted to see angels was to bolster their feeble faith. While I suppose this was a noble enough venture, it did little to satisfy the fact that there was a great big hole in my seeing gift, where the point should be. The only time I consistently felt good about what I saw was when I'd sit in the back of the church and talk to God about what was happening.

Jesus said that His disciples were not slaves but friends and that sharing what the Father was doing was evidence of this shift in relationship. I came to the realization, after twenty years of ignorantly stumbling around the spirit realm, that the reason I can see in the spirit is God wants me to know what He's doing.

If I own a business, I only need to tell my employees what they need to know to accomplish their job. It doesn't matter why. It doesn't matter what Dave over in accounting is doing. All that my employee needs to know is what I'm paying him to do. Asking too many questions is insubordination, and having an opinion is as likely to get you promoted as it is to get you reprimanded.

However, if my son goes to work for me, I will insist that he learn every aspect of the company. I'll answer every question he asks about how my business is run and listen excitedly to every comment and suggestion. Why? Because someday I want him to take over the family business. I am teaching him how to steward his inheritance.

God never wanted us to be His servants. He wants us to be His kids. Do kids serve their parents? Yes. However, their reason is very different than that of an employee. An employee serves so that he or she can get something. It is an exchange of time for money. A child serves because of the relationship he or she has with his or her parents. It is the impartation of legacy. And God wants you to know how His kingdom works so that wherever you go, you will re-create it.

Seeing in the spirit is fun. I enjoy seeing hordes of angels soar through the air to the sound of worship. I love telling people about the gifts that surround them. But all those joys are fleeting if I don't connect them with the kingdom and King they came from. Every spiritual gift exists for the sole purpose of bringing us closer to God. They are all in service of continual intimacy with Him. I was dissatisfied with my seeing gift until I realized that God was taking me on a tour of His kingdom—my inheritance.

At the beginning of this book, rather than giving you a gift, I wanted to open a door. The truth is that I hope to point out that the door has already been torn open. Jesus died so you could know God better—so you could be alone with Him without sin being the elephant in the room. There is no longer any barrier between His goodness and our hearts. He tore down the veil. Learning the magnitude of that goodness is our Christian walk.

This is how I know that seeing in the spirit is for everyone. Sure, you may not see as much as I do, and many of you will see a great deal more. But that's not really the point. The point is that Jesus opened the gates to the kingdom of heaven so that you could come through them.

I learned something the day I saw that girl get saved in a cattle auction house in England. There is more to be seen than any one or any thousand privileged individuals could ever contain. Seeing isn't a privilege; it's your destiny. I saw enough in a few youth kids at a conference to transform my life forever. There are too many people, too many blessings, and too much kingdom for only a select few to see into its depths.

APPENDIX A

FOR FURTHER STUDY

YOU MAY HAVE noticed upon finishing *The Veil* that for a book written by a Christian, targeted at Christians, about a Christian subject, there were surprisingly few direct references to the Bible or specific scriptures. Since the publication of the first edition of *The Veil*, the low number of scriptural references has been the chief concern of most people who have had a hard time with the book, which have been far fewer people than I expected while I was writing it. I intentionally included very few scriptural references, and there are still very few in the main body of this second edition; however, after receiving a few good suggestions, I found that I could supply a much stronger biblical basis for some of the concepts in this book without violating the original vision for it. Thus, this appendix was born.

I wrote *The Veil*, start to finish, three times. The first two versions were totally fine. They had plenty of Scripture references throughout. They presented my experiences in a clear-cut and dry manner. They attempted to partner each story and experience with a well-reasoned explanation of purpose. They tried to take each experience and make it applicable to the personal lives of anyone who might be reading them. And they were completely boring and lifeless. After finishing each version, I sat in frustration, saying to myself, "How did I make seeing angels sound so boring?"

Upon reflection I realized that while the first two versions of *The Veil* were factual and accurate, they were not at all *true* to the experience of seeing in the spirit. The way I grew into my gifting was not clean and straightforward. It didn't all make sense. Very few things that I saw came with a clear and immediate explanation; in fact, there are several for which I have still received no explanation. My conversations with the Holy Spirit on the subject, while peaceful and comforting, didn't follow the straight lines of logic or even the loose order of traditional narrative flow. It all just happened, more than I was ready or able to understand.

So I set out, on my third attempt at writing a book about seeing in the spirit, to write something that was true to my experience with the gift. The end product was very different from the first two versions. It was messier. It brought up more questions than it answered. It made few attempts at grounding anyone new to this subject. It left a lot of room for misinterpretation and misunderstanding. But it was the truest picture of the gift of seeing in the spirit that I had ever written.

While I am happy with how the book turned out, I am aware of the weaknesses caused by my approach. I only felt right including scriptures in the places where they would naturally occur in a conversation about seeing in the spirit. I am not an argumentative person by nature, and I almost never make any attempt to prove or validate my gift, so it didn't feel right to do so in the book.

Almost every time I added a scripture somewhere, it felt out of place, like I was trying to throw in qualifiers or justifications for my stories. It felt inauthentic, and it hurt the pace of each story. Unfortunately, it also feels inauthentic to my deep love and personal history with the Bible not to include more references to Scripture.

The following appendix feels like the perfect compromise. It is a separate section with a different tone. It doesn't break up the natural and conversational flow of the main body of the book. But it does give me the opportunity to share my thoughts and opinions on a few biblical references to the spirit realm. This is not an exhaustive study on biblical accounts of angelic activity. This is not an attempt to biblically prove the validity of my claims. This is just a few of my favorite verses about the spirit world with some brief thoughts on what they have meant to me over the years. They are little anchor points where I have noticed my experience matching up with those of men and women in biblical history, as well as guiding lights on the path to understanding all the wonderful things God has done and is doing for us.

> For in him all things were created: things in heaven and on earth, visible and invisible, whether thrones or powers or rulers or authorities; all things have been created through him and for him.
> —Colossians 1:16

This is one of my favorite scriptures about the spirit realm. Sometimes people think of the physical realm and the spiritual realm as different places, that they are separate. While this is true in one sense, it is also true that both the physical and spiritual realms are part of creation. God is bigger than both of them. They were both created for Him and by Him. It is a great reminder that all of the invisible world is meant to be seen and understood in the context of relationship with Him.

> Then the LORD spoke to Job out of the storm. He said: "Who is this that obscures my plans with words without knowledge? Brace yourself like a man; I will question you, and you shall answer me. Where were you when I laid the earth's foundation? Tell me, if you understand. Who marked off its dimensions? Surely you know! Who stretched a measuring line across it? On what were its footings set, or who laid its cornerstone—while the morning stars sang together and all the angels shouted for joy?"
>
> —JOB 38:1–7

This is another great scripture that reveals the context we should have for the spirit realm. God is speaking to Job, declaring the truth of His power and might, showing that He is not just bigger than the earth, but bigger than the realm of the spirit itself. It is also a good window into angels' personalities. They are shouting for joy, so excited at the amazing works that God is doing.

I have always been greatly humbled by angels' reverence and affection for God and the things God does. Whether by the subtle markers of posture and eye contact or by explicitly jumping for joy and celebrating, angels always honor what God is doing. It reminds me to pay attention so that I can more fully appreciate all the good that He is releasing every day.

At the resurrection people will neither marry nor be given in marriage; they will be like the angels in heaven.

—MATTHEW 22:30

But those who are considered worthy of taking part in the age to come and in the resurrection from the dead will neither marry nor be given in marriage, and they can no longer die; for they are like the angels. They are God's children, since they are children of the resurrection.

—LUKE 20:35–36

These are both interesting snapshots of the nature of angels. Though, as I have mentioned, I see angels that look masculine or feminine, I have never considered them to be male and female—not in the same way we are, anyway. I have seen angels that look old and I have seen angels that look young, but I never got the impression that this meant anything about age in the way we experience it.

Seeing an angel that looks old is more an indication of that angel's personality and character. It is a picture of the wisdom, confidence, surety, and dependability that come from years of experience. Younger angels are often carrying the vitality, flexibility, boldness, and creativity that are the hallmarks of youth. This, of course, doesn't mean that an angel that looks old can't also be creative and bold, though those traits may take on a new and different meaning when shown through an older-looking angel rather than a young-looking one. It is all part of the highly nuanced visual metaphor that makes up the way each angel looks.

> Each of the four living creatures had six wings
> and was covered with eyes all around, even under
> its wings. Day and night they never stop saying:
> "'Holy, holy, holy is the Lord God Almighty,' who
> was, and is, and is to come."
>
> —REVELATION 4:8

The Book of Revelation is full of beautiful heavenly imagery. Living creatures, six wings, eyes all around them; it all sounds so otherworldly. Yet what are these creatures doing? Worshipping God. Declaring His goodness. I chose this particular verse because it is a great example of something that sounds very strange and abstract, yet its purpose and focus is on God. It reminds me that no matter how confusing or unusual the things we see may be, we are meant to understand them by how they relate to our Father. It is then that their purpose becomes clear and they begin to seem much less strange.

> Then I saw another angel flying in midair, and he
> had the eternal gospel to proclaim to those who
> live on the earth—to every nation, tribe, language
> and people.
>
> —REVELATION 14:6

I like this one because when I read it I get the same feeling I get when I see an activation angel. As I mentioned in their section of the book, activation angels carry the opportunity to see God's will done on the earth. I see these angels all the time, carrying many different kinds of things, some so good that you would not believe they were obtainable or even possible. I think a big part of our Christian mandate is to grow into people who can see what God is doing and hear what He is saying so that we can release His kingdom on Earth.

> In the same way, I tell you, there is rejoicing in the presence of the angels of God over one sinner who repents.
>
> —LUKE 15:10

This is another wonderful picture of the personalities and values of angels. It can be so easy to forget that heaven is on your side, that every one of your victories is celebrated. We can sometimes get cynical about scriptures like these, imagining angels rejoicing just because it is their job or giving sarcastic applause to our meager victories, but this has never been true to my experience. Angels are nothing if not genuine. They laugh with you, cry with you, and celebrate your victories as if they were their own.

> It was revealed to them that they were not serving themselves but you, when they spoke of the things that have now been told you by those who have preached the gospel to you by the Holy Spirit sent from heaven. Even angels long to look into these things.
>
> —1 PETER 1:12

Angels have a different relationship with God than we do. I don't think I would necessarily label it as greater or lesser, just different. I mentioned earlier, in the "church" section of this book, a moment in worship when all the angels left. I have seen this happen several times, though I wouldn't call it common. Each time it happens, I feel the character of worship change to one of great intimacy.

I don't know exactly what the difference is between our relationship with God and the angels' relationship to Him, but I do know that we are greatly privileged to be invited into the depths of His presence.

> But you have come to Mount Zion, to the city of the living God, the heavenly Jerusalem. You have come to thousands upon thousands of angels in joyful assembly.
>
> —HEBREWS 12:22

> Then I looked and heard the voice of many angels, numbering thousands upon thousands, and ten thousand times ten thousand. They encircled the throne and the living creatures and the elders. In a loud voice they were saying: "Worthy is the Lamb, who was slain, to receive power and wealth and wisdom and strength and honor and glory and praise!"
>
> —REVELATION 5:11–12

People are often surprised when I tell them that I see five or six angels in their house. "Wow," they say, almost in disbelief. "There's that many?" I am often equally surprised that they didn't expect more. I am not sure where this idea comes from. It may be that people think that there aren't really enough angels to go around, or that they don't merit a strong angelic presence. Both are completely untrue. I have seen several hundred thousand angels in my lifetime. I have seen tens of thousands in one place on occasion. There is no shortage of angels. It is also important to remember that your merit is not based on the mistakes you have made or victories you have won; your merit is based on the value that God put on you—and He deemed you worth the blood of His only Son. Sending five or six angels is a small gesture for something that valuable.

> See that you do not despise one of these little ones.
> For I tell you that their angels in heaven always see
> the face of my Father in heaven.
>   —MATTHEW 18:10

Even though this is a subtle example of Jesus referencing what I call personal angels, it carries a lot of the nature I have seen and experienced with them. I often describe the relationship between personal angels and their person like something between that of a sibling and a parent. They are with us for as long as we are on this earth. They have seen the good, the bad, and everything in between. But without exception, every personal angel I have seen has a deep and profound love for the person they are with. The gentle warning Jesus gives here fits perfectly into the loving and protective nature I have seen in personal angels.

> So Peter was kept in prison, but the church was earnestly praying to God for him.
> The night before Herod was to bring him to trial, Peter was sleeping between two soldiers, bound with two chains, and sentries stood guard at the entrance. Suddenly an angel of the Lord appeared and a light shone in the cell. He struck Peter on the side and woke him up. "Quick, get up!" he said, and the chains fell off Peter's wrists.
> Then the angel said to him, "Put on your clothes

and sandals." And Peter did so. "Wrap your cloak around you and follow me," the angel told him. Peter followed him out of the prison, but he had no idea that what the angel was doing was really happening; he thought he was seeing a vision. They passed the first and second guards and came to the iron gate leading to the city. It opened for them by itself, and they went through it. When they had walked the length of one street, suddenly the angel left him.

Then Peter came to himself and said, "Now I know without a doubt that the Lord has sent his angel and rescued me from Herod's clutches and from everything the Jewish people were hoping would happen."

When this had dawned on him, he went to the house of Mary the mother of John, also called Mark, where many people had gathered and were praying. Peter knocked at the outer entrance, and a servant named Rhoda came to answer the door. When she recognized Peter's voice, she was so overjoyed she ran back without opening it and exclaimed, "Peter is at the door!"

"You're out of your mind," they told her. When she kept insisting that it was so, they said, "It must be his angel."

But Peter kept on knocking, and when they opened the door and saw him, they were astonished.

—ACTS 12:5–16

This story is so funny and relatable. People sometimes think that because I see in the spirit, I understand all the mysteries of the universe and have infinite divine knowledge. Not so much. Most of my journey with seeing in the spirit has been one of slowly developing faith and trust that the Holy Spirit will lead me to do what I am supposed to do with the things that I see.

I love this story because half the time no one is sure what's going on. Peter thinks he is just seeing a vision. He doesn't even realize he is experiencing a miracle until it's already over. Peter's friends don't believe he is at the front door. It's a twelve-verse spiritual comedy skit.

This is a wonderful lesson for anyone who is working on developing the gift of seeing in the spirit. It isn't always going to make perfect sense right away. You may not be entirely sure what you are seeing or what you should do about it. Thankfully, heaven is on your side and God knows who you are and how you think. He will give you exactly what you need to do what He's called you to do. Even if an angel needs to strike you on the side to get your attention.

As a small side note, this story also has a few interesting parallels with my experience. I have often seen personal angels that look just like the person they are with. Peter's friends brush off Rhoda's claim that Peter is at the door by saying, "It must be his angel," which implies that they would expect his angel to look and sound just like him. Another interesting note is that it seems that it was more plausible to them that Rhoda would be hearing Peter's angel than it would have been for Peter to be freed from prison. It makes me wonder how normal seeing in the spirit may have been for the early church.

> Amid disquieting dreams in the night, when deep sleep falls on people, fear and trembling seized me and made all my bones shake. A spirit glided past my face, and the hair on my body stood on end. It

stopped, but I could not tell what it was. A form stood before my eyes, and I heard a hushed voice: "Can a mortal be more righteous than God? Can even a strong man be more pure than his Maker? If God places no trust in his servants, if he charges his angels with error, how much more those who live in houses of clay, whose foundations are in the dust, who are crushed more readily than a moth! Between dawn and dusk they are broken to pieces; unnoticed, they perish forever. Are not the cords of their tent pulled up, so that they die without wisdom?"

—JOB 4:13–21

Here is an interesting account of Eliphaz, the speaker in this portion of the Book of Job, having some kind of spiritual encounter. He sees something, but he is not sure exactly what it is. The message sounds like it may be from God—Eliphaz seems to think so—but it is not especially clear. I like this example because sometimes when we see in the spirit we don't see the whole picture. Even to this day, sometimes I will see an angel that is so blurry I can't make out any distinct features. Sometimes I will hear something but I am not entirely sure it is from God.

This is a very important thing for people who are getting started with seeing in the spirit. There is a good chance that for a while, a good portion of what you see may be unclear. You may not understand what you are seeing or what you should do about it.

It is stories like these that remind us how important it is to have a group of healthy and well-rounded people speaking into our lives, people whom we can bounce our spiritual experiences off of and get direct and honest feedback. It creates a safe place to grow, and it will accelerate that growth even more.

> In the past God spoke to our ancestors through the prophets at many times and in various ways, but in these last days he has spoken to us by his Son, whom he appointed heir of all things, and through whom also he made the universe. The Son is the radiance of God's glory and the exact representation of his being, sustaining all things by his powerful word. After he had provided purification for sins, he sat down at the right hand of the Majesty in heaven. So he became as much superior to the angels as the name he has inherited is superior to theirs.
>
> For to which of the angels did God ever say, "You are my Son; today I have become your Father"? Or again, "I will be his Father, and he will be my Son"? And again, when God brings his firstborn into the world, he says, "Let all God's angels worship him." In speaking of the angels he says, "He makes his angels spirits, and his servants flames of fire."
>
> But about the Son he says, "Your throne, O God, will last for ever and ever; a scepter of justice will be the scepter of your kingdom. You have loved righteousness and hated wickedness; therefore God, your God, has set you above your companions by anointing you with the oil of joy."
>
> He also says, "In the beginning, Lord, you laid the foundations of the earth, and the heavens are the work of your hands. They will perish, but you remain; they will all wear out like a garment. You will roll them up like a robe; like a garment they

will be changed. But you remain the same, and your years will never end."

To which of the angels did God ever say, "Sit at my right hand until I make your enemies a footstool for your feet"?

Are not all angels ministering spirits sent to serve those who will inherit salvation?

—HEBREWS 1:1–14

This is a great snapshot of the government of heaven. Angels are not meant to be worshipped, obviously, but they are also not meant to be ignored. Their services are part of the inheritance of salvation. We are meant to receive the benefit of their presence in our everyday lives. They are here to help us do what God sent us here to do:

For he will command his angels concerning you to guard you in all your ways; they will lift you up in their hands, so that you will not strike your foot against a stone.

—PSALM 91:11–12

Praise the LORD, you his angels, you mighty ones who do his bidding, who obey his word. Praise the LORD, all his heavenly hosts, you his servants who do his will.

—PSALM 103:20–21

"If you are the Son of God," he said, "throw yourself down. For it is written: 'He will command his angels concerning you, and they will lift you up in their hands, so that you will not strike your foot against a stone.'" Jesus answered him, "It is also written: 'Do not put the Lord your God to the test.'" Again, the devil took him to a very high mountain and showed him all the kingdoms of the world and their splendor. "All this I will give you," he said, "if you will bow down and worship me." Jesus said to him, "Away from me, Satan! For it is written: 'Worship the Lord your God, and serve him only.'" Then the devil left him, and angels came and attended him.

—MATTHEW 4:6–11

One of the chief purposes of angels is to serve God and His children. I think one of my main goals with this book is to illustrate how many wonderful and beautiful ways God has equipped them to do that. We are covered in every possible way, protected from every possible angle, provided with every resource, and surrounded by the support of heaven.

APPENDIX B

RECOMMENDED READING

For ADDITIONAL UNDERSTANDING on seeing in the spirit, I recommend the following resources.

- *The Seer* by James Goll
- *The School of the Seers* by Jonathan Welton
- *Angels* by Billy Graham

NOTES

PART II: ANGELS AND INFINITY
PEOPLE

1. "Current World Population," Worldometers, accessed July 27, 2017, http://www.worldometers.info/world-population/; "World Birth and Death Rates," Ecology.com, accessed July 27, 2017, http://www.ecology.com/birth-death-rates/.

ABOUT THE AUTHOR

BLAKE K. HEALY is one of the senior team members at Bethel Church of Atlanta in Georgia. He is also the director of the Bethel Atlanta School of Supernatural Ministry. He lives in Peachtree City with his wife, April, and their four wonderful children: Haydon, Finnley, November, and Ender. For more information, or to contact Blake, visit blakekhealy.com.

bassm

BLAKE K. HEALY, author of *The Veil*, is the director of the Bethel Atlanta School of Supernatural Ministry. At BASSM Blake and his team train revivalists who hear the voice of God, know their heavenly identity, and operate with supernatural power and authority. If you would like to grow in the prophetic ministry, see signs, wonders, and miracles, learn more about seeing in the spirit, and grow closer to your heavenly Father than ever before, then visit bethelatlantaschool.com for more information or to apply for the upcoming school year.

Your life will never be the same.